MW00459581

THE RAGING SLOTH

THE RAGING SLOTH

An Upside-Down Blueprint to Bust Your Limits,
Build Your Purpose, and Balance Your Life

Eric Eaton

ISBN: 978-1-943526-35-2 (paperback)
ISBN: 978-1-943526-34-5 (hard cover)
Library of Congress Control Number: 2016908742
Author Academy Elite, Powell, OH

The Internet addresses in this book are accurate at the time of publication. They are provided as a resource. Eric Eaton and the publisher do not endorse them or vouch for their content or permanence.

To protect the privacy of those who have shared their stories with the author, some details and names have been changed.

Author Photography: Rebekah Reiger, www.snapbeck.com
Cover Design: Tehsin Gul

For Erica, thanks for your support, strength, and inspiration, and for allowing me to become a *Raging Sloth*.

CONTENTS

Foreword ix

Introduction 1

Part 1 Bust Your Limits – Getting Off the Ground

1 The Sloth's Predicament 13
   Being Comfortable in Your Own Skin

2 Life Getting Turned Upside-Down 27
   The Disrupting Obstacles in Your Journey

3 Denying Your Limitations 39
   Living Life Like Nothing is Wrong

Part 2 Build Your Purpose – Making the Climb Toward Success

4 Step One: Engaging Your Limitations 55
   Confronting Your Obstacles to Gain Success

5 Step Two: Defining Success 69
   Defining Success on Your Terms

6 Step Three: Knowing Your Passions 91
   The Pitfalls and Promises Behind Your Passions

7 Step Four: Adjusting Your Habitat 103
   Finding Your Way Back Home

8 Step Five: The Fellowship of the Raging Sloth 113
   Building Community For Your Journey

9 Step Six: Entering The Danger Zone 127
      Taking Intentional Risks

10 Step Seven: Shifting Weight 143
      Learning to Be Flexible and Giving Yourself Grace

11 Step Eight: Owning Your Inner Raging Sloth 157
      Becoming the Best You

12 Step Nine: Eliminating Excuses 169
      Never Having to Say "I'm Sorry"

Part 3: Balance Your Life – Life in the Tree

13 The Balance of the Raging Sloth 183
      Achieving Effective Balance in Life

14 The Serious Business of Play 207
      Resurrecting Your Fun Side

15 A True Raging Sloth 219
      Commitment to Working Hard

16 A Lifelong Raging Sloth 231
      Thinking Long-Term

Conclusion: Living an Upside-Down Life 235

Appendices

   Discussion Questions 241

   Acknowledgments 251

   Endnotes 253

FOREWORD

I don't think we're all meant to cruise through life at the same speed. I think some of us were meant to go fast and others slow. It's easy to judge and critique, but petty practices like these rarely produce anything productive.

I think the key is to run your own race and at your own pace. Easier said than done. And that's why *The Raging Sloth* is so needed. Think of it as a much needed guidebook. Here's why.

Most people want to experience a successful and abundant life. But is this possible in a world full of pain and obstacles?

The Raging Sloth provides a positive blueprint on how to move forward, even through the muck and mire of life.

Speaker, author, and leader Eric Eaton shows you a 9-Step process to:

- Engage your obstacles and leverage them to experience victory

- Find purpose in the midst of your own limitations

- Redefine success on your own terms

- Live a life free of guilt, frustration, and excuses

Through his own journey Eric reveals his constant struggle with chronic pain *while* pursuing success in every part of his life. Through these highs and lows, Eric learned his entire life could thrive *in spite* of his pain, but only if he redefined success on his own terms.

Eric shows how anyone with limitations can live the upside-down life of success by becoming what he refers to as a "Raging Sloth."

Isn't it time you became a Raging Sloth and bust through your limits, build your purpose, and balance your life? The Upside-Down Life is a life worth living.

Kary Oberbrunner
CEO of Redeem the Day and Igniting Souls
Co-creator of Author Academy Elite
Author of *Day Job to Dream Job*, *The Deeper Path*, and *Your Secret Name*

INTRODUCTION
But it's my destiny to be the king of pain.
~ The Police

"I do not have what it takes!"

This was the hardest confession I have had to make—humbly admitting I was at the pit of my life, living in a space I did not belong. I had to tap the mat and admit defeat.

The situation was not where I saw myself at this stage in my life, but I had no choice. I had to admit I could not go on, because if I kept living this false journey, then I would keep living a life that was slowly tearing me apart.

I had to admit I was a sloth; I was slower than the others and I could never keep up with the crowds. But in admitting I was a sloth, I began my transformation into a Raging Sloth!

THE RAGING SLOTH

What is a Raging Sloth, you might ask?

A very good question. This moniker was born out of a light-hearted description of my slow movements due to a life of chronic pain. It was a playful label bestowed upon me as the person always in the back of the pack. I do not move around

1

quickly nor do I run. There is a rule in our house that my children learned at a very early age. If they see Daddy running, they do not need to ask any questions—they need to start running, too. Daddy is being chased.

I've had to come to terms with the fact that I am a bit slower in my pace and cannot keep up with my more swiftly footed friends. But soon this characterization became more. The sloth, like me, did not choose to be slow, but the sloth makes the most of its circumstances. The more I unwrapped the description of a sloth, the more I knew I must make every day count and embrace my challenges in spite of my circumstances.

As I dug deeper into the intricacies of the sloth, I had to admit, it's really not the animal you'd want emblazoned upon your shield as you venture into a battle. Sloths are widely known as extremely slow animals who sleep most of the day.

The word *sloth* is listed as one of the seven deadly sins, which opens up another theological debate we'd do best to avoid here. The name "sloth" is also bestowed upon people who are deemed lazy, slow, indolent, and who love to sleep.

Slothful people are criticized as useless and worthless, and overall, the word has a negative connotation. Yet, against my better judgment, I began to be intrigued by this small, tree-dwelling mammal that always seems to have a smile on its face.

The more I researched the sloth, the more I realized it is simply misunderstood and carries some unfortunate labels. Even though sloths never asked to be slow or lethargic, that is simply the way they were made. For in reality, sloths are really good at being sloths.

Sloths have also survived for an extremely long time on this earth. Twenty-three different varieties of ancient sloths have been identified. The most notable was the ground sloth, which grew to the size of an elephant.

Sloths know how to persevere, adapt, and live in their uniquely suited environments, which is a trait I needed to understand better for myself. Suddenly, the label was beginning to make sense.

But I was not *just* a sloth, as this simplistic label did not exude the definition I had been struggling to identify with for years. I felt like I had the heart of a lion trapped in the body of a sloth. I had a burning desire in me to do more, but was restricted by the limitations of my body.

These two contradicting characteristics were reconciled in the transformation of becoming a Raging Sloth.

Raging is defined as "ardor; fervor; enthusiasm" and as "for being popular and fashionable." I had a fire inside me trying to ignite. I possessed a tremendous amount of fervor and enthusiasm, but it was trapped in my sloth body. I had to create space to allow these two traits to come unleashed, united in their journey.

Raging evolved out of a summer camp I have worked at the last ten years. I was introduced to raging by Steve Harrold, the founder of The Knights of Heroes Foundation. Steve is an amazing individual who created a camp for boys and girls who have lost their fathers in military service.

I have the utmost respect and admiration for Steve and the endless energy he pours into others and this camp. He is an inspiration to what hard work can accomplish. But Steve is definitely a cheetah, and I spend most of the time attempting to keep pace with him.

During the week of camp, we go rock climbing, river rafting, hiking, and downhill mountain biking; we throw tomahawks, and shoot archery. When we are out on our micro-adventures, we are raging—we're having a blast, giving every activity all the energy we possess. No one holds anything back, even to our bodily detriment.

During this one week out of the year, both the campers and the mentors are living life to its fullest. This passion and fire that exude out of me during this time demonstrate how I should be living my life all year long. I need to unleash the raging side of me.

You also may be a sloth, by virtue of some unrequested challenge or obstacle placed upon you. But you are going to live this life with everything you have, and you are going to expend all the energy you have to enjoy this life. Why? Because it is the only life you have, and you are going to live it with all the passion and fire you can generate.

The unofficial subtitle to this book was going to be, "Circumstances Suck! Life is Great. Let's Make it Awesome," because we all have situations we do not desire placed upon us. I may not get to choose how my body feels on a daily basis, but I do get to choose how I am going to live my life, regardless of my circumstances.

EMBRACING MY INNER RAGING SLOTH

In order to choose how I was going to live, I needed to embrace my inner Raging Sloth!

I had resisted because for eighteen years, I had small glimpses of hope. I thought the next surgery, the next round of physical therapy, increased medication, or maybe more rest would provide the relief I desperately desired from my chronic pain. Then I could get my life together and jump back into the corporate rat race to achieve success like my peers.

Only it never happened. I have spent my adult life in chronic pain, starting with hip dysplasia in my early twenties. I opted for corrective surgery which caused nerve damage down my right leg. While the surgery reduced the pain in my hip, it did not entirely eliminate it and has left me suffering every day of my life.

I endure bad days and worse days. The good days, physically, are few and far between. But I kept on trying to keep up with the crowds. I kept trying to be "normal." I desperately tried to keep in the race. I was unknowingly grasping for a definition of success in my career and my personal life, which was not mine.

Attempting to live a life in which I could never succeed, I would push the pain down into a dark hole within my soul, grit my teeth, smile—because you always have to smile—and pretend everything was fine.

I would sit in meetings in a distracted daze, trying to comprehend a client's problem, or attempting to be patient with coworkers who were unaware of what I was burying inside, and having the realization I had little control over my life and career.

Part of my resistance was my manly pride; I did not want to admit to myself or anyone else that I was incapable or even disabled. I was adamantly fighting being labeled "disabled." I was also resisting people's dreaded sympathy.

The looks of "Oh, poor you" did nothing for my confidence or ability. It was always this certain look in a person's eye, when they tilted their head slightly and looked at me like a sad puppy dog. Even though I knew people meant well in their hearts, it was not a response I desired.

I was extremely afraid that if I honestly admitted the depths of my pain and struggle, no one would look at me or care for me the same as before, or that I would be treated as something less. I have always been a big, strong, and able individual, and part of me did not want to admit I might not have what it takes. I never wanted to admit I might not be able to finish the job or was not up to the task.

I had a great job with great pay, worked with great people, and had a career track that would ensure a very comfortable retirement, but I was miserable—partly in the sense like everyone else who doesn't feel they are working a job that fills their soul. But this was more. I had to admit I did not have what it took physically to successfully work this specific job.

It became evident to me one night while sitting in a restaurant with several partners and directors enjoying a late meal after a successful sales pitch. As the individuals at the table were discussing their jobs, their clients, and their responsibilities, it became clear to me in this moment that my physical restrictions would be a barrier for my success if I continued in this field.

I did not have the ability to keep up with this crowd. After years of hip surgeries, hip pain, limping, and nerve damage, the constant pain was physically limiting my ability to run with the big dogs. But on days of extreme pain, I was also mentally and emotionally exhausted because of the toll the pain exacted.

I do not get to decide when to bring my A game and give it my all. I do not get to decide my level of pain when I wake up in the morning. Most days on a client site, I am extremely weary by the end of the day simply from attempting to keep up with my colleagues and the client. How could I be successful in my career if what I was seeing unfold was the only definition of success?

What I was beginning to understand is I would have to turn the definition of success on its head and create a different version of success for myself.

Since I don't get to choose my good or bad days, I simply have to wake up, take the day as it comes, and do my best to make the most out of each day.

Even though I do not get to choose how I feel when I wake up, I do get to choose what I do with the day. So I choose to be the best I can be. For it is in this moment that I can begin to create a better adventure.

JOINING THE ADVENTURE

The Raging Sloth provides a pathway to live a successful life on your terms, in spite of your challenges, obstacles, or limitations. You are going to have to look at life differently, but life might turn out better than you could have dreamed or imagined.

This is where the Raging Sloth was born, beginning as a joke—from feeling like I was moving and living my life in slow motion to the realization that I could be a great sloth. I have amazing gifts, talents, abilities, and experiences to contribute. But they need to be developed and used in my own environment, employing my skills and talents appropriately.

I could have simply succumbed to the sloth title and lived my life sitting in the recliner. This is where I am most comfortable and experience the least amount of pain. But I have a raging desire to succeed, to live life to its fullest, to help others, and to be the best version of me I can be. I have the fire within me, and with a little intention and purpose, I know I can thrive in my own environment.

This is not the story of a person who went through one issue and came out on top. This is my journey of high mountaintops and deep, deep valleys over the course of an eighteen-year period...and counting. The majority of this book was written from the recliner in my living room. For I was in too much pain to move or function in a normal capacity.

Through this process, I was constantly attempting to figure out how to live life while enduring constant pain. I have made many mistakes and failed along the way. But I keep getting up because life is beautiful when you can live it on your terms, regardless of your circumstances.

The Raging Sloth is a guide, a way to clear a path for you to become the best version of you possible in spite of your obstacles. Through my own experiences, research, and personal failures, I have created a path to succeed, not just in my career, but also with my family, relationships, and life in general. I've learned how to adapt to create a better life physically, mentally, and emotionally, and to live with a deep spirituality in spite of the constant pain I endure.

This is why we are called Raging Sloths. We are a community of individuals who are not content to live the life given to us, but take life on our terms. We may not take it quickly, but neither are we content to settle for a life of pain and suffering. We have a fire within us to do more, to make ourselves better and make the world around us a better place.

Every day is an obstacle, and every day I choose to engage this obstacle. Because even though I live in pain and life can be a challenge, I choose to make the most out of the life given to me. This is the story of the Raging Sloth.

PART 1

BUST YOUR LIMITS:
GETTING OFF THE GROUND

1

THE SLOTH'S PREDICAMENT

Being Comfortable In Your Own Skin

**All our dreams can come true, if we have
the courage to pursue them. ~ Walt Disney**

You have a dream.

You at least have some expectation or desire about how life
should evolve. This is how you were designing your life from
a very early age. You have these dreams bursting from inside
you.

A dream to be a musician, dancer, or CEO, start your own
company, raise a family, make a lot of money, write a book,
run a marathon, or create the next great product. Our dreams
are God-given gifts to live an adventure beyond our imagination and see it become a reality. You can probably immediately recall the dream that constantly tugs at your heart?

The problem with dreams is that they are fragile. When
you have placed a variety of expectations upon your life to
achieve something amazing, it takes very little to shatter

those delicate ideas. There are too many unforeseen factors precariously holding your dreams like an exquisite vase.

The other unfortunate aspect of dreams is that life will get in the way. You get married, buy a house, and get stuck in the job you didn't want out of college but needed to pay off all your school loans. You keep telling yourself after a couple of years that you will stop and pursue your dream.

Children come, more bills pile up, and you are promoted to a respectable position in your company. Or you are pouring yourself into your children hoping to provide stability and promise.

The dreams you had bursting inside of you suddenly get tucked neatly away in the back of your heart, only to be taken out periodically for you to wax nostalgic over missed opportunities.

This is a daily struggle for most people. Unfortunately, this struggle becomes magnified for individuals who are living with some type of uninvited limitation or obstacle. It puts you in the unfortunate situation of not even knowing what you could have accomplished, what you could have attained had you been whole.

This is your predicament. You feel trapped somewhere between your dreams of what life was supposed to be and the reality of the obstacle you are facing. No one writes this story, no one provides a roadmap for this adventure, and there are very few guides to help you along the way.

But this is your life. This is your existence, and your current reality. The question becomes *what do you do*? How do you live with your limitation? How do you define success? How do you live a "normal" life on a daily basis?

This is your struggle. This life was never what you had planned or what you had imagined, but it is the reality of what you are living.

A "PAINFUL" REALITY

Life, as we all know, can be challenging enough. When we add in navigating relationships, finding a career, pursuing a passion, and learning how to relax, we can become overwhelmed very quickly. Each year, this internal battle we engage in becomes more and more complex to navigate. Let's look at our lives in general:

- 67% of the American population is optimistic about the future compared with 89% internationally. This number has been decreasing steadily over the last few years in America.

- We are more disentangled and disingenuous with our relationships.

When it comes to our careers, Dan Miller in his book *48 Days to the Work You Love*, quotes the following statistics:

- 70% of American workers experience stress-related illness.

- 34% think they will burn out on the job in the next two years, according to the U.S. Department of Health and Human Services.

- There is a 33% increase in heart attacks on Monday mornings, according to the *Los Angeles Times.*

- More people die at nine o'clock Monday morning than any other time of day or any other day of the week, according to the National Center of Disease Control and Prevention.

- There is a 25% increase in work-related injuries on Mondays, according to *Entrepreneur* magazine.

- Male suicides are highest on Sunday nights, with men realizing that their careers—and possibly their finances as well—are not where they want them.

Most people in America are not living a life they can even manage, let alone the life they dreamed. They are challenged by the realities of life and career. Then you add in the following issues of people suffering from chronic pain:

- According to the American Pain Foundation, about 32 million people in the U.S. report having had pain lasting longer than one year.

- Other research suggests the number is closer to 50-100 million American people are suffering in chronic pain.

- From one-quarter to more than half of the population that complains of pain to their doctors is depressed.

Lasting chronic pain can cause the following side effects:

- Anxiety

- Frustration

- Anger

- Depression

- Low self-esteem

- Loneliness

- Fatigue

- Diminished concentration, critical thinking ability, and productivity

Radha Chitale, when discussing pain for ABC News in an article titled *How Chronic Pain Gets Into Your Head* states, "New research by scientists at Northwestern University in Chicago may explain why people who have chronic pain also suffer from seemingly unrelated problems such as depression, anxiety, lack of sleep and trouble focusing. The study showed that people with chronic pain have a portion of the brain that is always active: the region associated with mood and attention. This constant activity rewires nerve connections in the brain and leaves chronic pain sufferers at greater risk for mental problems.

"How you identify yourself to others is an important element of your individuality, and having chronic pain and not knowing when it will go away, if ever, is a huge issue that can change the course of your identity. If you are experiencing chronic pain, you might not be able to do certain tasks or fulfill certain roles that were once common, and that can feel disempowering."

When you are suffering in pain and trying to live a "normal" life you are not doubling your problem. You are multiplying your issue as your frustration and anxiety about your work life balance are exponentially amplified. This is why you can no longer simply live your life. You have to make a change; you are required to live life differently or else your life will explode.

This is not a situation where you rise above the pain or the limitation. You don't have the luxury of raising your arms in victory because you overcame your obstacle. There are too many forces working against you.

But you can rise above the circumstances of the pain or limitation. There is a pathway out, a pathway to success, a pathway to freedom, a pathway to living life abundantly. But it will look nothing like what you dreamed of, which is the beautiful part.

RECONCILING THE SLOTH'S LIFE

This is the sloth's predicament, for the sloth did not request its current state of slowness. When God was handing out qualities and attributes to all the animals, I doubt the sloth was relaxing in its recliner, eating grapes, having the peacock fan him with its feathers, stating, "I see you gave the cheetah lightning speed. That seems like too much work; I will take the opposite."

Nevertheless, this was how sloths were created; they are slow. In fact, sloths are so slow they have a greenish tint to them because of algae growth in their hair due to their lethargic movements. Sloths sleep longer than most mammals, show little excitement, and certainly do nothing expediently. But despite all of these seemingly negative qualities, the sloth is an animal to be admired.

Let me tell you why. It goes back to the dreams and expectations in your life, this deep desire in you to succeed. You want to succeed on some level in your life: in your relationships, at home, in your current career, or in an exciting new venture. Everyone has some goal in mind, some expectation of a life they want to pursue or live.

These dreams are God-given desires that come from being His creation. You were not created for status quo nor to simply exist. You were created for greatness, to change the world, and to make an impact on this world.

God chose specifically to partner with you to see His kingdom realized on this earth. I believe this is what drives you and moves you forward in your pursuit of a greater life.

Because you are a creation, when you are at your best, you will move toward greatness. When you are allowed to roam freely in your own habitat, you will change the world. This is evident by the many great organizations we have serving this planet to make it a better place.

The predicament arises when you are creating your dreams. In your dreams, you are viewing yourself as normal. You exist and fit in like everyone else; this is a central part of the dream. But when life becomes abnormal, you no longer understand how you fit into your dream.

This lack of normalcy makes you feel trapped. And when you feel you do not have a choice, you will move toward depression and self-destruction. You will let the hurt, pain, and challenges of life dictate how you should live, because you have resigned yourself to simply accept your fate.

You will let your limitations obscure your direction and purpose because you do not think you are worthy of anything else or capable of greatness. Yet the sloth, who really should not even exist, keeps going, keeps surviving, and keeps thriving, even though it was given substantially less than other animals.

This is why it is so important to keep your focus on what you can accomplish, your good qualities, and your abilities instead of what you missed, what you are incapable of doing, or what you lack.

Lingering negative thoughts only create frustration over the kind of life you could never have lived nor able to live. In reality, the life you dreamed of may not have been enjoyable, but for some reason you hold onto this idea like a child to her favorite toy.

But what if there is a reality out there far greater than what you could have imagined and it is due to your limitation? You see, you are not normal; you're what Malcolm Gladwell calls an "outlier." In his book *Outliers*, Gladwell looks deep into the lives of people who did things out of the ordinary to tell us "people don't rise from nothing."

You are not simply born into success but cultivated through your life and circumstances to embrace success. And the obstacles you have faced in your life have created a phenomenal foundation for your success—because you are not normal. Your limitation makes you an outlier, if you are willing to engage in the transformation.

MY PREDICAMENT

Like any child, I grew up having dreams. I wanted to be a great husband, to be an awesome father, to work hard at a cool job, and to be successful in my work so I could prosper financially. And I was off to a good start.

Out of college I accepted a professional job, learned business process design and systems programming, and moved quickly into the consulting world. By my early twenties I had persuaded Erica, a wonderful woman, to marry me before she had too much time to consider her options. I was working at a great job and making more money than any of my peers—which was ironic since I graduated with the lowest GPA of anyone I knew. Life was good.

But this career path was not my dream. It was the dream that was placed upon me out of tradition. You grow up, go to college, get married, get a job, buy a house, and live happily ever after. There were many holes in this model, but it was all I knew.

The circumstances were not bothersome because I was suc-
ceeding in this plan. Oddly, I believe I could have lived out
this reality for the rest of my life without a problem if an
obstacle had not been placed in my path.

My dream began to get cloudy when one day I began to
experience a sharp pain in my right hip. I did not think much
of the pain at the time. I would simply muscle through it like
I always had and move on with life.

There was too much positive momentum in my career to let
anything get in my way. I convinced myself this was a speed
bump in my pathway to success. Soon it would be over, and
I would get back into my career and kick it into high gear.

Only it never went away. Multiple surgeries never removed
the pain and created more damage in other areas. I was left
with severe nerve pain that would dramatically change the
trajectory of my life.

My fragile dreams shattered in an instant. I would spend
years desperately searching for ways to put the broken
pieces of my dream back together.

REWRITING THE EPIC ADVENTURE

Eventually, it became evident I could no longer put this
dream back together. In order to succeed in my life, I was
going to have to rewrite the modern narrative for myself to
create a better adventure.

There are no grand tales being told through generations about the heroic exploits of a sloth. The sloth does not invoke the image of an epic adventure. Otherwise, it would be a very long, drawn-out adventure. But the narrative could change with the Raging Sloth.

You are mesmerized by these types of stories because of an inner desire for greatness. When you read or watch an epic tale of a hero on a quest, you lose your thoughts in the journey, imagining yourself to be the one living the adventure, slaying dragons, saving the day, and...well, being the hero of the story.

It is an age-old formula that Hollywood has been using to draw moviegoers to the cinema for years. There is really nothing magical about the tale itself, but the unfolding of the story taps into those inner desires you have to achieve greatness.

Even within real life, when we see a news story, social media post, or movie about someone who overcame all odds to succeed, was miraculously healed, or overcame their inner pain to win, we let out a collective cheer. We love it. We want to see more and be drawn into these stories as they pull at our heartstrings while tapping into this inner desire.

We cheer on Peyton Manning coming back from a neck injury to win the Super Bowl. We are enthralled by Captain Sully and his lifesaving efforts to land a damaged plane, against all odds, on the Hudson River. We are moved by author J.K. Rowling's rags-to-riches story in the creation of the *Harry Potter* series. We are captivated by Louis Zamperini's story, which was told in the movie *Unbroken*, of how he endured a grueling concentration camp in Japan during World War II.

The storyline is based on the foundational aspect of the hero OVERCOMING the obstacle in the tale. Their success is dependent upon this storyline—Manning winning the Super Bowl, Captain Sully successfully landing the plane, Rowling's books becoming wildly popular, and Louis Zamperini being set free from the concentration camp to create an amazing life. The story is the hero *overcoming* the pain or struggle in their life to achieve greatness.

But what about those "heroes" who do not have the opportunity to overcome the pain or obstacle? The reality is that the hero does not always get to go on the adventure, slay the dragon, and save the day.

What happens when you come across this storyline? When you do not get to move on from the pain, the suffering, or the challenge? These are stories rarely told, but they are just as important to intertwine into the modern narrative.

When the hero does not "succeed" by our modern standards, what happens when they go back to their little kingdom? It is in these instances we need to rewrite the adventure. The story needs to change from a formulaic product to something much greater.

When you get back to the kingdom after a seemingly failed adventure, it may be time for you to find a new environment where your adventure can continue.

But this time it will be on your terms. Your adventure will be written down in the words of your choosing. You are a hero, but you become the hero through your own choices because you choose the adventure despite the obstacles you face. You become the hero not because you overcame your obstacle, but by engaging the obstacle head-on.

This is the story of the Raging Sloth, a story desperately ringing in your heart of a better adventure you long to live—because it is your adventure, and one where your dreams dictate the epic, heroic ending.

FINDING MY OWN ADVENTURE

Early on in my career I was creating my perfect adventure. I fortunately got the girl, but I did not save the day. When I returned to my kingdom, it did not look the same and I felt out of place. This in fact was not my adventure at all. It was written for someone else, someone with different capabilities, desires, and dreams.

I needed to find my own adventure, my own life, which would be more in tune with my abilities and limitations. But I could not find a roadmap, and there was no guide. I had no idea where to go or what to achieve.

Though I stumbled many times, this started me on the greatest adventure of my own life in search of where I truly belonged.

I needed to become The Raging Sloth.

2

LIFE GETTING TURNED UPSIDE-DOWN

The Disrupting Obstacles in Your Journey

In this world everything is upside-down. That which, if it could be prolonged here, would be a truancy, is likest that which in a better country is the End of ends. Joy is the serious business of Heaven. ~ CS Lewis

Emily had the perfect life. She was married to Rob who served in the Air Force, and they had two amazing little kids they were raising together. Having known each other since high school, they were married shortly after graduation. They attended college together and after four years of late nights and term papers, they joyfully graduated with their diplomas. Rob joined the Air Force, and the couple persevered through basic training and Rob's first two deployments.

Life was finally getting into a place where they could enjoy a familiar routine. They were about to move into their dream house. Emily was figuring out life and was living the dreams she had always imagined. All the hard work from college to watching Rob endure basic training; from the long nights waiting through two deployments and raising two kids by herself as Rob served his third and final tour. In a very short period of time, life was only going to get better as they enter a brand new stage of their lives.

Until Emily received the knock on the door no spouse in the military wants to hear. The knock that hits you like a shot of adrenaline, ignites every nerve, and makes every hair stand on end. The knock that appears as a dream and makes your entire body go tense as an overwhelming and terrifying pit explodes in your stomach.

Rob was gone. Emily had lost her husband to an IED in Afghanistan as he was being transported to a different base. In an instant, her life was turned upside down, her dreams shattered.

Emily was suddenly a single mother who had to navigate life on her own. She had to figure out the litany of processes to jump through in order to receive benefits as a military widow. She had to raise two kids on her own. All the questions began rolling through her head—who will show their son how to be a man? How to tie a tie, change a tire, or how to treat a girl? Who was going to show their daughter the character of a man and let her know she would always be daddy's little warrior princess?

Sometimes life turns us on its head, and we have no other way to respond but to begin to live life upside-down. For this is the only way our circumstances can begin to make sense.

LIFE UPSIDE-DOWN

One of the more defining characteristics of a sloth is they do everything upside-down. They eat, sleep, mate, and even give birth in an upside-down position. As a result, their fur grows in the opposite direction, away from their extremities and with a parting on the tummy. The upside-down life of the sloth is how they adapt to make the best use of their environment and existence. It is also how they have kept safe from predators and managed to thrive when in reality, they should have become extinct a long time ago.

As much as I do believe that religiously and constitutionally all men and women are created equal, we are certainly not all created the same. But this is what makes us so amazing, because it is not how we were created which makes the difference; what matters is what we do with our time. We are different.

We all come in different shapes, sizes, strengths, intellect, thought processes, and passions. And that is absolutely wonderful. The broad stroke God used to paint mankind is what makes us kind, serving, humble, innovative, and amazing. Out of the box we're not all going to do things the same way. We look at problems differently, we function differently, we have different energy levels, and we run head on into life differently. Some people even need to live life upside-down in order to see this life appropriately.

THE BEGINNING OF PAIN

I began to notice a pain in my right hip, which would occur intermittently. The pain would come, usually from a long walk or spending the day on my feet, but would go away after a night's rest. The first real flare-up occurred when my wife and I were visiting her college roommate in New York City. We walked for miles—going to Broadway shows, eating at diners, and taking in the sights. That night was really the first time I remember the pain being a little different.

When I went to bed, the pain was sharper than usual, but eventually I was able to get some sleep. In the morning, the pain disappeared and we were on our way again. I was not paying it much attention nor did I tell my wife what was happening, mainly because I did not know myself.

A few months later I began a Project Management role in San Diego, enjoying the beautiful sunshine and magnificent ocean views. I was working on a long-term project in the downtown area and was flying back and forth from our home in Northern Virginia.

One of the first weekends in San Diego, I went on a long walk with a colleague down Mission Beach to enjoy the sunshine. It was such a beautiful day, we kept on walking without paying much attention to how far we had travelled. The day was almost perfect with very few reasons to go inside.

When I went back to the hotel at night, I noticed the same pain I felt when I was in New York City. Again, did not think much of the pain, simply took some Advil, laid back down in bed, and assumed it would be gone in the morning.

Only when I woke up, it wasn't gone. The pain *stayed*. It really stayed. For the next several months, the pain grew progressively intense in my hip and groin area.

I began the process of seeing different doctors and ortho-pedics to get their opinion on what I was experiencing. At twenty-six years old I began using a cane, because the pain of simply walking around became too much. The doctors would prescribe me medications to dull the pain, which didn't accomplish much except to dull my mind and senses. It was the first time in my life I felt like I was living someone else's life while walking in their shoes. What was happening to me was surreal at best.

One doctor diagnosed me with hip dysplasia. It was a bit strange to realize my pain was caused by something I had my entire life. It explained a lot—I was the only kid over six feet in high school who could not dunk a basketball. I could never run as fast as other kids my age and size. I just assumed I was slow. But there was an underlying medical issue I didn't know existed.

The solution for the injury was a surgery where they would cut my pelvis in three places and rotate it around in order to give more coverage to my femur bone. I was somewhat ignorant of the invasiveness of the procedure. Still young, and somewhat naïve, I treated it as if it was just like any other trip to the emergency room. I simply wanted to get it fixed so I could get back to work and keep climbing the corporate ladder of success.

The surgery lasted for more than eight hours because the doctors ran into more complicated issues than expected.

Like breaking the bone saw while trying to cut my hip (take that Wolverine). Post-surgery, I was put into a room with heavy dosages of morphine to knock me out and keep me stable.

After a couple of days in the hospital, they came in and began the process of installing the body cast. I was completely unprepared for what was about to happen. The doctor and nurses began to put a cast on me, which started from my chest down to both ankles. For stability, a bar was placed between my knees.

Completely wrapped up and ready to go, they put a bow on me and called an ambulance to deliver me back to my house. I am the only person I know whose first ride in an ambulance was from the hospital to their house and not the other way around. At home, we had acquired a hospital bed for my use. I could also raise and lower the bed, which was pretty much my complete range of motion.

For the next four weeks, I was completely at the mercy of friends and family. I could not move and was incapable of taking care of myself. I had to rely on people to feed me, bring me drinks, and help in going to the bathroom. If I dropped the TV remote, I was stuck with whatever was on until someone could retrieve it for me.

This time period was a completely humbling and humiliating process all in one. When my wife and I got married and she said, "For better or for worse," I'm not sure she was prepared for what she was going to have to endure.

But it was about to get worse.

Over the course of the next couple of weeks, I began to notice a slight electrical shooting pain in my right foot. At first it felt like my foot was falling asleep. But by the next week, the pain grew in strength and intensity. Soon my foot felt like it was on fire, as though someone had hooked a car battery to my big toe, sending electrical currents pulsating up and down my entire leg. The doctors were giving me more morphine and medication to help me sleep and try to alleviate the pain. But nothing worked.

It finally became too much and we called the ambulance again to take me back into the hospital where the doctor removed the cast. While the cast was gone, the damage, either from the surgery or the cast, remained. Somehow, my peroneal nerve had been irreversibly damaged, and I would have to deal with chronic nerve pain from my big toe to the top of my hip for the rest of my life.

This was the point where my life began to turn upside down. It was not a quick turn, like a knock on your door, or a call from your doctor. It happened over the course of several years and it snuck up on me. Because it was so slow in its movements, I resisted the upside-down life. I was always holding out hope for healing or something to alleviate the pain. I was not paying attention to the fact that my life was becoming something I did not recognize.

TAKING A DIFFERENT VIEW OF LIFE

When you have a physical, mental, social, or emotional obstacle on top of the daily grind, to say life is challenging is an understatement. You want to be successful, you want to create something new, you want to light a fire in your soul, but you feel held back by your limitations. You can also feel inadequate because you don't fit the normal molds you see all around you. You think your limitations are holding you back or keeping you from your dreams.

You may also struggle with thoughts such as: *Why did this happen to me? Why am I burdened with this limitation?* You ask the question, "If only I was like____" and then you fill in the blank with the type of sports figure, musician, artist, friend, or businessperson you wished you could emulate. These thoughts can drag you down and cause confusion if you continue to look at life through everyone else's lens but your own.

Over the next couple of years as I was going through physical therapy, injections, medications, acupuncture, and pain blocks, I could slowly see my soul and existence begin to slip away. I no longer understood where I belonged.

My physical activities were limited. The medications and pain made my mind wander, foggy, and brought me into a deep state of depression. I did not want to be around others because I did not want to hear about how much fun they were having, or see their faces as they looked at me with unwanted sympathy.

I no longer understood or could find my place in life. Everything I was passionate about and cared for in my past no longer held interest to me as I was constantly looking for relief from the pain. My biggest issue was trying to fit a round expectation of life into a square hole of my reality. The two were incompatible; they could no longer exist together. I needed to take a different view of my life if I was going to do more than survive.

CHANGING MY PERSPECTIVE

This is why, just like the sloth, I needed to turn my life upside down and begin to live life differently. The sloth, even though it was born with certain limitations and restrictions, had learned to adapt with what was given to him and make the most of his life. I was slowly coming to the realization that my life would never be like it was or like I dreamed. My life would also never look like anyone else's I knew. Nor would others really understand the true depths of my pain and suffering.

To thrive in this life, you need to adapt; you need to make a change as you begin to look at life differently. When you are made to live life upside down but are constantly trying to live like everyone else, you are creating a recipe for disaster. It will cause confusion and frustration as you constantly try to make two realities co-exist, which were never meant to be together. Like attempting to mix oil and water together, it will never happen no matter how much energy you put into the process.

You will never be able to function in a manner deemed "normal" by other people—but that is awesome. You were meant to live upside down, and now you need to figure out how to turn your life in that direction.

This has been my struggle and frustration for many years—living in pain and struggling with how it affected my life. I worked exceedingly hard to succeed and try to fit in with everyone who lived right-side up. I had to master the art of masking my pain. Much like a functioning alcoholic, or more appropriately, a *functioning painiac*. I could go into the office or meet a client even while in a tremendous amount of pain, suppressing it to get through the day.

But all I was doing was getting through the day. The majority of my energy was spent trying to prove to everyone else that I wasn't in pain. In reality, I wasn't giving a very stellar performance at my job. It was difficult to concentrate, and I did not have the brain power to think through problems, which ordinarily would have been easy for me.

Having to meet a large group of people or sit through day-long seminars was draining. If I was on the road I would go straight to my hotel room after work and pass out. Masking my pain throughout the day was an exhausting exercise and was not benefiting anyone, least of all myself.

Through this time, I was truly trying to live someone else's life. I was trying to be someone I was not, which is exhausting to begin with, but even more so with a limitation. It was in these times wherein I started to write more; I also started to do some public speaking on pain and challenges, which marked the beginning of learning how to live life on my terms, upside-down.

I found that, even on my worst days, writing had become my escape. When at work I could not look at a spreadsheet and comprehend what I was viewing, but I could sit down and whip out a few thousand words of a story with ease.

Writing was effortless, and for a brief time, I could lose myself in words and forget about my pain. It did not matter whether anyone would ever read one word I wrote, I was discovering something about myself. Or, in some cases, rediscovering what life looked like when lived on my terms. I did not realize it at the time, but I was beginning to see what life looked like when you accepted your status of living life upside down.

A funny thing happens when you begin to live upside down. You get this vague sense of comfort. A sense like this is where you belong and how you were created to live. This is the reason why you were uncomfortable before, because you'd been living a right-side up life. It made you uneasy, frustrated, and confused.

At first, you couldn't put a finger on it nor describe the root cause, you simply knew something was wrong. It is like Neo in the Matrix, knowing something is not right, but unable to comprehend the problem. So you continued to live life as you knew it and spend your nights trying to discover what you are missing.

So when you finally find your voice, when you find your life-line and begin to live the way you were created, you start to get a sense of how you should approach life. When you live upside down, you begin to see the vivid colors of the world on the brilliant canvas it was meant to be seen.

If you want to be successful—and we will look further at how you define success—then you have to change your view and your perspective on life. You have to stop trying to live the way other people are telling you to live, opting for a life more suited to your environment. Which means you need to stop listening to what other people are telling you, and you need to grab on hard to that branch to hold on tight while living upside down.

Once you accept your upside-down position, you can begin to clearly see your wants, desires, and passions, and your limitations will no longer seem so limiting. The curse of being a sloth is that if we continue to try and live like everyone else, it is like dying a slow death. But if we can change our perspective, see life from a different angle, we can begin the process of becoming a Raging Sloth and move toward success and life on our terms.

3

DENYING YOUR LIMITATIONS

Living Like Nothing Is Wrong

To regret one's own experiences is to arrest one's own development. To deny one's own experiences is to put a lie into the lips of one's own life. It is no less than a denial of the soul. ~ Oscar Wilde

Tracy had always been determined with big plans, from early on in high school earning two straight bids to state championships in track to earning a scholarship running track in college. Tracy has always run hard on the track and in life, giving every task her complete and undivided attention.

Tracy graduated at the top of her class in her MBA program and was making waves in a high-profile marketing firm in New York City. She still had time to jog daily and would run races on the weekends if time permitted.

It was at one of these races that she met Steve. They would eventually fall in love and get married. Tracy was continuing to impress in her career and was moving up the ladder even ahead of her schedule.

Life was even more enjoyable because she could come home in the evenings for a run with Steve. They also took many weekend trips to the countryside together. Tracy was beginning to feel invincible.

The pain and discomfort Tracy would begin to feel did not come on suddenly. It started with sore muscles, which Tracy simply attributed to her inconsistent jogging schedule.

With more responsibility at work, she was unable to stick to her routine. Then she began to get restless at night and was unable to sleep. Over time she felt a tingling sensation in her legs, feet, and hands.

It was at this point that Tracy decided to see doctors. They were dumbfounded and would simply prescribe various pain medications and send her home. Her life was slowly transforming. There were no more jogs, evening dates with Steve, or weekends in the country. Tracy could barely survive a day at work. Because of the pain and lack of sleep, her thoughts were not as clear as before and she was not performing like her old self.

After eighteen months of going to different doctors, Tracy was diagnosed with fibromyalgia. Tracy could not believe it and Steve did not know how to respond.

She was healthy. She had always been active, running track in high school and college. How could she be diagnosed with such an ailment? Would she ever get better? Could she get back the life of her dreams?

DENIAL AND THE FALSE JOURNEY

A sloth is perfectly maximized for only the minimum necessary actions during any given day due to the fact that its metabolism and muscle mass are half the rate and size of other animals of equal proportion. It is absolutely important that they know and understand their limits in order to not waste much-needed energy engaging in unnecessary tasks.

For those of us with obstacles in our way, it is very important that we not only know and understand our limits but that we work within those limits. If you are going to change and become an efficient Raging Sloth, then you must be committed to knowing yourself better.

The obstacles you face in life can come in many forms and can become major obstacles very quickly. The limitations can include: having physical pain, physical limitations, lack of energy, emotional stress, or mental limitations, being a parent of a special needs child, or simply not having a type A personality.

Your limitation can be anything placed upon you that you neither asked for nor wanted, whether through unforeseen circumstances or a poor twist of fate. But you have no choice but to deal with it directly.

When you deny or ignore your limitations, you are creating massive problems for yourself that you may not be fully aware of. There will be confusion on your work choice, your relationships, and your life in general, which will result in you lying on the floor in the fetal position, a blubbering mess. This occurs because you are walking down a path you are incapable of living, in pursuit of a life that denies your limitation.

When you do not know yourself, when you have not taken the time to really review your life from an introspective standpoint and be honest about what you see, you will begin a false journey.

A false journey is taking an adventure or pathway meant for someone else. The road looks appealing at the onset but will eventually create confusion and frustration.

On your false journey, you will listen to the words of friends, family, professors, bosses, doctors, or spouses and think what they say is the correct course of action for your life. The problem is you have not taken the time to discover how your dreams conflict with your limitation, and this denial is keeping you from success.

When you do not know your own limits, you can begin to go on many false journeys that may not be necessarily destructive, but at the very least, can cause confusion and frustration. When I was denying my limitation, I did not know it at the time but I was heading for a brick wall at a very accelerated pace.

THE BEGINNING OF DENIAL

Fourteen years after my hip reconstruction, my hip had fully degenerated to the point that I needed a replacement. This was what I had been waiting for. This was my final hope. I was certain that after the hip replacement, the pain in my hip would go away and I would have more functionality— I'd be able to live my life more freely, the way I thought it should be lived.

The replacement surgery went about as well as expected. The doctor put everything in the correct place and the hardware was holding up steady. I started rehab, and I was on my way back to success and living a life I thought would lead to happiness.

But a few months into my physical therapy, my rehab began to stall. I was not gaining strength like I should have been, and the pain was not going away as quickly as I thought it would. I was also battling an unexpected weakness through-out my entire body.

During routine exercises, I felt that if I had a monitor on my body showing my energy level, you could watch it drain within seconds. This weakness and lack of energy was as much emotionally draining as it was physically. I should have been getting better, not stalling in my recovery.

Contributing to the malaise of pain and confusion, I strug-gled with work efficiency. Attempting to be an engaging Senior Pastor at church while dealing with personal pain proved to be very trying.

When I was suffering, it became increasingly difficult to be a shepherd to a group of people. The pain and struggle of trying to keep my own life straight became too unbearable.

I had very little energy for my wife or kids, who had endured more than a family should over the prior year. This left almost no energy or interest for the needs of people inside the church.

The easiest path to pursue while in denial is to ignore the problem and simply run. Run as fast as you can without looking back (I mean that metaphorically as I still can't run). So that is what I did. I quit my job at the church, packed up the family, and moved to Arizona to start over thinking this would solve all my problems.

The move did help my healing. I started working at a corporate job again, and no one was any wiser about my previous health issues (except when I could not get through the metal detector at the airports). I could isolate myself enough from the rest of the world and simply heal.

The healing part was good; it would take me about two more years to feel at least 80% normal from the replacement surgery. But the isolation cut much deeper than any surgery, and it took me many more years to recover.

In the midst of this denial and attempting to live my life like everyone else, I switched consulting firms and began working for a very high-powered global firm. When I first started working in my position I was feeling better than I had in years.

The pain was low, I was getting stronger, and I felt comfortable with my knowledge in my role. I could finally regain my position back in the rat race. It was time to take the next step in my career.

The biggest setback at this point was the metal detector sounding off every time I went through the airport because of the metal in my hip. It was like the TSA had identified me as a covert spy. I became very adept at knowing which metal detectors I could get through at which airports. While that is another story about TSA consistency, I still believe if you set off the metal detector you should at least get to choose which creepy attendant is going to pat you down. I have been patted down more than any man who has never committed a crime. But I digress.

While I was gaining more momentum during this portion of my life, I thought I was finally getting everything in order. All the sacrifices and pain were behind me, and for the first time I began planning out my future and what I would be doing until retirement.

Then a new pain began to manifest in my hip and groin. At first I thought it was just from the travel—the long flights, sitting all day in a conference room, and nights in hotel rooms. I tried to suppress it and tried to deny it, but my mental power alone could not distract me from the pain.

I started going to doctors—getting shots, attempting another round of physical therapy, and getting all types of scans and injections to find the problem. Nothing was making it better, nor were the doctors able to tell me exactly what was causing the pain. All the while my job was moving forward at 100 mph.

THE GRADUAL TURN

This was the beginning of an epiphany in my life. The darkness began to disappear, the fog clearing away as I realized I was denying my limits. This denial was having an adverse effect on my choices, my health, my relationships, and my life.

I knew I had talents, abilities, and gifts I could use. I knew I could make an impact and difference through my experiences and knowledge, but not in this place and not in this context. Over time, what I was learning about my body and my limits was that I could get a lot of work done, but it had to be on my terms and my timing.

Part of my definition of success is also to be present for my wife and children. They've endured enough because I was not the man I thought I could be or the father my children deserved. Traveling down this path of denial, I was denying them the most.

I was not present most of the time because I was on the road, and when I was home I was in too much pain to really engage or even care about their problems. This was not who I wanted to be or my idea of a successful family, but it was an area of my life I knew I could change for the better.

Through many doctor visits, it was discovered that there were many different issues happening within my hip and body which all needed to be addressed separately. Because of this, I never knew how I was going to wake up in the morning. I had no control over what type of day would unfold.

There were days when I'd wake up well and feel fine, but by noon the pain would return and become a major distraction. There were also days when the physical therapy was too overwhelming, and I would go home to lie in bed until the excess pain rescinded.

No matter how well I awakened, I was exhausted by the end of the day. I would make minor adjustments and do my best to give my family what they deserved, but my tank was being drained quickly and constantly.

The pain and discomfort became so overwhelming at one point that I finally could no longer travel for work. The little gift during this time was that the company did not know what to do with me because I could not travel. I also could not give them a clear understanding of exactly what was wrong and how it could be corrected because I was not receiving a clear diagnosis for my pain.

The company kept bouncing me back and forth between people, trying to find me some place to engage in until the pain became so intense I finally had to go out on short-term disability. It was during this time that I put my head down to fully dedicate myself to writing. I was not going to take this pain lying down, literally or figuratively. This is the raging side of me—I could not sit idly by and do nothing.

I was coming to the realization that my physical pain was not going to change. I think sloths move faster than my awareness, but my life needed to change dramatically. Pain was a constant reality, and I needed to deal with it appropriately and stop denying my limitation. I knew that if I was going to survive I would have to survive on my terms, and I was finally willing to give it everything I had to succeed.

I realized that if I worked on my schedule, on activities which brought me life, it would address the fire in my heart. I'd wake up early to work on these tasks. If I was having a good day, I could work all the way through the day and be very productive.

On the other hand, if I was having a bad day, I'd try to work in a nap, or at least lie down for a bit, put ice or heat on my hip, or take a hot shower. On certain days, being able to break up my day allowed for more productivity.

I had freedom and flexibility to be able to work around my limitation, to be as productive as I could be throughout the day. I had been unable to experience this in the past, and only through this hiatus I was given did I see its benefits.

I could schedule my meetings at times that I found typically worked better for me. This is very difficult when you are at the mercy of someone else's schedule. Deadlines and project requirements become increasingly challenging when your body does not want to cooperate.

It was not until I was able to work through this schedule that I saw the importance of really knowing yourself and understanding your limitations—not so you can stop doing what you are doing, but so you can work more effectively and efficiently around your limitations.

TO THINE OWN SELF BE TRUE

This will be the point in your life where you have to be overly committed in learning all you can about yourself. You need to understand your body, soul, and mind. You need to understand how food, exercise, sleep, medication, alcohol, and social activities affect you.

The more you can become dialed into your own body and the rhythms of your life, the better you will be able to respond to your environment. Otherwise, you will only be reacting to what is happening around you.

For example, too much sugar in my diet kept me from having the energy I needed throughout the day. I was also being dragged down by gluten. I did not have terrible reactions to it, but as I began to streamline my life I came to understand that whenever I ate gluten I felt a little bit off, so I needed to eliminate it from my diet.

It was the same with alcohol; when I drank a couple of glasses of wine I felt like the alcohol would seep into my bones the next day. It was not worth the drink to make my limitations worse. I had to be in tune with my body and watch over what I was putting into it that made me feel worse.

On the flip side of this, through physical therapy, I learned I was not stretching or strengthening properly and had not been for years. Now I was learning to open up my body more so the pain was not as difficult to deal with and, when I did feel the pain come on, I could take a break and do some exercises or stretches in order to keep the pain at bay and get my body to feel better.

My morning exercises have almost become my ritualistic cup of coffee. I need to do them or I am not the same.

These are coping methods you need to explore for yourself. What makes you tick, what opens you up, and what closes you off? What foods are you putting in your body? What habits are you practicing that are not healthy or are not contributing to your success? Are there exercises you should be doing both physically and mentally, or breathing exercises that can help calm you down and improve your focus?

This by no means is going to be an easy task. It takes time, dedication, and devotion, but nobody cares about your success more than you, and the benefits are well worth the commitment.

Committing to learn more about yourself and understanding your limitations are really the first steps in moving toward success. Learning more about your limitations will help you know which careers, jobs, and even relationships you probably need to avoid, as well as those you need to gravitate toward. More importantly, it helps you understand how you can live a successful life.

What type of environment is best suited for your physical, mental, or emotional state? Do you work better at night or in the morning? Do you need to stand up or sit down more, or maybe a combination of both?

This understanding can open up doors and opportunities you have never thought about before. It can also eliminate the tremendous amount of frustration stemming from your efforts to be successful in spite of or by ignoring your limits.

By denying your limits, you will stay on an unhealthy and frustrating false journey. You will be living someone else's life and constantly trying to be someone you are not, and you will never find joy or fulfillment this way.

You will constantly be side-tracked by trying to be someone you cannot physically, mentally, or emotionally mimic. Eliminate this frustration by taking the time to explore your limitations and see how you can be abundant and productive as your own Raging Sloth.

PART 2

BUILD YOUR PURPOSE: MAKING THE CLIMB TOWARD SUCCESS

4

STEP ONE:
ENGAGING YOUR LIMITATIONS

Confronting Your Obstacles To Gain Success

Life is either a daring adventure or nothing at all.
~ Helen Keller

The first time Sandi encountered pain it was enough to take her breath away. Sandi was in shock. She was in her early twenties, spent most days in the gym, competed in body-building contests, and ran stairs and swam laps with energy to spare. But the pain in her back and knees would put her in bed for days. Eventually, the darkness and depression crept up on her in a way she wouldn't wish on anyone.

Sandi said, "For many years, my identity became that pain. 'I have (fill in the blank) and can't do that.' It was the 'reason' I gave for not being able to go places, chase my dreams, live out my goals. It's easy to get to that place. And you slip into this identity struggle where now you're saying 'I AM my condition' and not 'I HAVE a condition.'"

But Sandi refused to live in this place of darkness and identity confusion. She rose above the pain to create a twenty-million-dollar empire. Her business A Real Change provides wisdom and direction to small business owners. Sandi said that the "big difference now is I choose to live a life of joy and not surviving."

Engaging in the litany of doctor visits, medications, advice from friends, and naturopathic experimentation, Sandi had been able to keep the pain under her control instead of letting the pain control her life. She realized that no one who had never experienced extended chronic pain would ever understand her situation, and she accepted the fact that "everyone has an opinion, but YOUR opinion is the only one that really matters."

TRAGICALLY HIP

Even though sloths did not choose to be one of the slowest, most dormant animals on the face of the earth, they still have to work with what they were given. They do not spend their days attempting to mimic other animals. I bet you have never seen a sloth auditioning for a lion, a platypus, or an elephant.

They are sloths, and they have uniquely adapted to their given situations as sloths to maximize their time and energy. They do not have the energy, nor do they need to try to be any other animal than a sloth.

How often in life do we attempt to be someone or something we are not? Even though we are walking around with an obvious limitation, we try to pretend it isn't there and live with a mask on pretending to be someone else. Maybe we have never dealt with our limitation properly, or we deny its power over us, or we simply are using it as an excuse.

I lived many years under the assumption that my hip would eventually get better. I thought that once I got my hip replaced then I would be fine, the pain would go away, and I could get back to my perceived definition of success. Because I was always hanging onto this belief that I would someday get better, I was denying what I was dealing with on a daily basis. You would think after eighteen years I would get the hint, but now you know the incredible thickness of my skull.

When the pain eventually returned, it was a wake-up call that made me realize I no longer recognized my surroundings. The biggest issue at this point was I had moved so far out of my own habitat that I started to panic at realizing I was so far from my reality. I had tried to live another life, be another animal, wear another mask for such a long time I almost believed I was meant to live right-side up.

But you can only live this way for so long. In the midst of pain, your heart's true chord will eventually begin to ring louder and louder. I knew something was wrong. I knew I was missing something essential to my soul. There was a pit in my stomach telling me I was off course. But I could never quite put my finger on the reason, mainly because I had never taken the time to figure out the "why" of the pit.

When we moved back to Colorado, I began to realize I was living the wrong way. It was similar to having the feeling of waking up after a deep sleep not really knowing where you were—only this time, I did not know how I got there or what I was going to do to get back home.

This entire time, all eighteen years of it, I had been attempting to hide my limitation. I was trying to pretend it didn't hurt and that it didn't affect how I lived my life or the choices I'd been making.

How or why my wife put up with me this long and didn't hit me over the head with a frying pan is beyond me. It was pretty obvious to her that something was not firing on all cylinders, but this is one of the struggles people like me face.

One of my greatest challenges during this whole time was my refusal to embrace my limitation. I was Igor limping around the neighborhood, carrying a gigantic bag on his back and telling everyone, "Keep moving. There's nothing to see here." Because of my hope of healing and getting better, I never wanted to fully admit this was going to be my existence.

What was not obvious to me, was glaring to those around me. If I was going to move forward, if I was going to be successful and live my life upside down, then I was going to have to embrace my limitation and learn to live life engaging my obstacle head-on.

I am not saying that I needed to embrace my pain—that would be masochistic—but I needed to come to terms with my circumstance and accept it for what it was so I could move on with my life. I think this was difficult for me because there always seemed to be this ray of hope on the horizon that all of this would go away one day. So I neglected what it was doing to me physically, how it was affecting my relationships, and how I was doing my job.

FINDING PURPOSE

I had to change my question from "When will this go away?" to "How do I embrace my limitation?" This is not an easy process or endeavor, but I knew it was paramount to breaking through to my success.

Ralph Waldo Emerson said, "Bad times have a scientific value. These are occasions a good learner would not miss." I needed to become a good student and understand the value behind what I was experiencing.

At the beginning of this enlightenment, my eyes were being opened. I do not believe in coincidences, but it was at this time I read several books in a row that all referenced the psychiatrist Dr. Viktor Frankl. I found it odd that in my previous readings, during a brief stint in a counseling graduate program, and research in therapy, I never ran across any mention of Dr. Frankl. But his name came up so much in these other books that I eventually read his book *Man's Search for Meaning*.

Dr. Viktor Frankl knew what he wanted to do in life from a very young age. Even in the early 1900's, he knew that he wanted to work in the field of psychiatry. Frankl was so sure of his profession that at the age of sixteen he wrote a letter to Sigmund Freud. Freud was so impressed by the letter, he had it submitted to the *International Journal of Psychoanalysis* to be published. It would not take long for young Viktor Frankl to establish himself as one of the greatest psychiatrists in Vienna during his day.

Unfortunately for Frankl, his day was during Nazi rule and prelude to World War II. Frankl was a Jew. It was only a matter of time before Frankl, his new wife, his parents, and everyone he knew were being held in a concentration camp in Theresienstadt. Frankl would spend the next three years in several different Nazi concentration camps until the camp he was incarcerated in was liberated in 1945.

But Frankl walked out of the camp alone; his wife, parents, and brother had all perished. Prisoners in the concentration camps were either dying from starvation or put through the gas chamber while serving in the camps. Frankl also learned that many of the prisoners had simply let go of life because of a general lack of meaning.

When Frankl left the camp, he returned to Vienna, and in a mere nine days wrote the book *Man's Search for Meaning*, which has become one of the most influential books ever written. When Frankl reviewed his time in the concentration camp, he observed a distinction between those people who had lived and survived the crisis and those who had died.

The difference, from his time in the camp, came down to one thing: *purpose*. He came to this conclusion through his own experience and by reflecting upon the words of Nietzsche, who said, "He who has a Why to live for can bear almost any How."

"Those who found meaning even in the most horrendous circumstances were far more resilient to suffering than those who did not," wrote Frankl in *Man's Search for Meaning*. "Everything can be taken from a man but one thing: the last of the human freedoms—to choose one's attitude in any given set of circumstances, to choose one's way."

In America, more than most countries, we struggle with the balance between meaning and happiness. We struggle to find meaning even in dire circumstances because we are too consumed with our lack of happiness.

We want to be happy, which usually has to do with financial success, health, and well-being. But we also want to have some sort of meaning in our lives. We want to know that the time we spend on this planet actually means something to someone.

This attitude is only magnified when you are living with a limitation. When you wake up every day in pain or suffering, getting out of bed can become increasingly difficult, let alone trying to take on the day. With a lack of purpose, we become enveloped in our own pain and miss sight of a greater purpose our lives can serve. This was the difficult lesson Frankl learned in the concentration camps.

Realizing my own lack of purpose was a slap in the face. I had little or no purpose in my life when it came to contributing back with my gifts and talents. I had spent many years teaching, serving, and helping others. I knew this was a passion and a gift, but I had set it aside during this time of my life. I convinced myself I had nothing to offer because of my pain.

To dull the pain I was drinking more than I should, numbing my mind with senseless movies and television, and basically turning myself off to everything around me in order to deny the existence I lived. I was using my pain as an excuse to dig a deep hole and hide from life.

My wife and children provided me a comfortable life during this time whether they knew what they were doing or not. But I needed to engage myself in work that possessed a greater purpose. Ironically, when I was engaged in something with a greater purpose, it opened up my eyes to the importance of meaningful relationships with my family and others.

Once I realized I needed to transform and be more productive, I knew I had to find my purpose. I had to engage my soul in life-changing work that would have a profound effect on others. This was what would eventually get me out of bed, to serve a greater purpose.

What you eventually have to come to terms with is the fact that your limitation may be the very experience in which you find your purpose. The very circumstance that makes you want to hide and that you believe has ruined your life may be the next door that is opening in your life. While one reality may have been eliminated when your obstacle appeared, another—and greater—reality may take its place.

I never enjoyed talking about my pain, and I never really wanted to talk to people in chronic pain (we tend to not be the most exciting crowd). I never enjoyed reading books on chronic pain, either. It was simply too depressing and not what I wanted to be doing with my life. Again, I was denying my purpose because I was denying my limitation.

But during the course of this time, when speaking publicly on a blog, podcast or some venue, my pain was by far my most popular subject. I substantially received more feedback and questions on pain than all my other topics combined.

I thought my purpose was more along the lines of teaching spiritual disciplines or using my corporate experience for small business development, but pain drew me in and was what piqued most people's interest.

Once I took the leap to put a more positive, hopeful spin on the problem of chronic pain, my purpose was born. I wanted to help people create a better adventure for their lives, to guide people to live life upside down and be abundantly successful in spite of their circumstances.

ENGAGING MY OBSTACLE

Finding your purpose allows you to embrace your limitation. Without it, I'm not sure this is an easy task to accomplish. Maybe you are different than me, but I have a tendency to become fixated on my pain and all it has stripped from me. Once you find purpose, you begin to see your limitation through a different lens, allowing you to embrace it and move forward in your life.

I cannot begin to imagine the atrocities endured by those like Frankl in Nazi concentration camps, every day wondering if it would be their last under inhumane conditions. But if Frankl, and others, can find their purpose in the most horrendous of circumstances, why can't I?

You embrace your limitation by engaging your obstacle. I use the word *engage*, because you do not get the luxury of *overcoming* your obstacle. I was getting tired of reading books or articles about people overcoming their obstacles to live a greater life. I do not get the luxury of overcoming my obstacle, but I *can* engage my obstacle.

You have a limitation that will not be healed, taken away, or changed. Your obstacle is not something you simply overcome, leave behind, and never see again. Your limitation is a part of your life, whether you like it not, and you cannot move forward unless you engage your limitation head-on.

While you cannot overcome your obstacle, you can overcome the circumstances of your obstacle. You do not have to live the life of a victim. You can learn to thrive in life instead of surviving. You can take charge of your life and live it extraordinarily.

Once I created time to reflect on my purpose and fully engage my limitation, it was extremely freeing. The pain didn't magically go away, but the burden of carrying the pain all these years did. I could see I was living the wrong way and

I needed to turn back upside-down to see life with greater focus.

I began to realize what I needed to be doing, where my passion lay, and the fact that I needed to do everything I could to get back up in the trees, to my habitat. Because if I kept on pretending to live on the ground, then I was bound for a slow yet certain death.

HOW TO ENGAGE YOUR OBSTACLE

If you are going to engage your obstacle head-on, the first step you need to take is to be honest. You need to be honest about what your limitation is, how it affects your life, and how it limits your activities. This may not all be bad, but you need to list those activities you want to do but can't. Be truthful about those activities you can engage in, but have avoided using your limitation as an excuse.

The next step is to be realistic about what your limitation means in your life. How does it affect your relationships, your career, your hobbies, or your interests? You need to be realistic about your healing and the effects of medication. Is there a long-term solution? Is your current reality as good as it gets for you? Being realistic about how your limitation affects you will allow you to create a better plan to live a better adventure in your own life.

The third step is to be a visionary. You have a limitation and you cannot live life like you planned, but who cares? What can you do with your life? How can you live it upside-down?

How can you use your limitation to help others? Think very far outside the box to find your own purpose in order to live life upside down in a truly amazing way.

The last step you need to take is to keep climbing. Engaging your obstacle means you fight no matter what. Your life is worth living and it is awesome. Do not let anyone else tell you otherwise.

When I was on disability I could have spent every day lying on the couch in my pajamas, watching Netflix, and feeling sorry for myself; instead, I was getting up at 5 a.m. every morning and doing my physical therapy, spending time in prayer, showering, and shaving.

I would put on my clothes like I was meeting someone for lunch every day, regardless of whether I was leaving the house or not. It was the one thing I could control and something that made me feel human. I avoided at all costs simply sitting around the house in my pajamas.

If you are suffering from pain or another limitation, you have to fight and climb every day. Get out of bed, shower, put on decent clothes, and attempt to interact with society. These are behaviors that are suggested for "normal" individuals to get out of a funk; how much more important are they for those of us who have to fight to get out of bed every day?

If you live like nothing matters, then soon you will believe that you do not matter. Nothing could be farther from the truth, but you are going to have to get up every day and engage your obstacle.

CHOOSE YOUR PATH

If you choose the path of the Raging Sloth, then you are going to have to engage your limitation with full force, whether your obstacle is physical, mental, emotional, or relational. Maybe you do not have an abundance of energy or a type A personality. That is all right. Don't try to change yourself (but don't make excuses if there is an area of your life you need to change).

Be realistic with what life has placed in front of you, engage your limitation, and climb back in the tree. This exercise may take getting some good close friends or family together and letting them be honest with you about how they have seen your limitation affect your life and their lives. It may be hard to take, but trust me, the outcome will be well worth it because you will finally be able to drop the mask to have a life you are called to live on your terms.

If you don't engage your limitation, then you will continue living your life like I did for so many years: looking beyond the horizon at something that would never come and living in someone else's shoes, suffering a slow death. Finding your purpose in order to embrace your limitation is the first step to finding your own success and living the awesome life of a Raging Sloth.

5

STEP TWO: DEFINING SUCCESS

Defining Success On Your Terms

Always be yourself, express yourself, have faith in yourself, do not go out and look for a successful personality and duplicate it. ~ Bruce Lee

When our oldest son Dylan was in eighth grade, he came home one afternoon and declared he was trying out for the school soccer team. In one sense I was proud of him for attempting such a lofty goal, but he had not played organized soccer since he was six. In this day and age of playing sports right out of the womb, his chances of making the team were slim.

My son is a very confident young man and I wanted to make sure realistic expectations were set. I took Dylan aside and explained how proud I was of him trying out for the team. But I also explained gently that he probably would not make the cut. Dylan would be trying out against other boys who have been playing soccer for years in a very competitive environment. I did not want him to be too distraught if he didn't achieve the success he desired.

Dylan reassured me he'd been playing soccer every day during recess with other guys on the soccer team. Although I was glad he was going into the tryouts with some experience, I did not see how playing soccer during recess could compare with playing on an organized team.

The tryouts were spread out over a couple of days and at the end of each day, he would tell us how he did and give us some of the coaches' feedback. When tryouts were over, Dylan came home to tell us he made the team. He was one of the last boys chosen, but he had made the cut. Dylan went on to practice every day, worked hard, and by the end of the season he was a starter for his school team when they won district.

Fast forward to his sophomore year and Dylan started on the varsity soccer team for his high school. You see, Dylan refused to let a definition of success keep him from attempting to do something he loved. He did not buy into the adage you had to play the sport from a very young age to make a school team. Dylan went out and redefined success for himself to create a space where he could thrive.

RADICAL MIND SHIFT

No matter how hard you try, you cannot turn a sloth into a very good dog. Can you imagine how excruciatingly painful it would be waiting for the ball to be returned during a game of catch? But the great thing about sloths is they don't try to be anything other than what they are, which is really awesome sloths. We can all think of an individual we admire, or are even a bit jealous of, because they are comfortable in their own skin.

In becoming a Raging Sloth, you need to make a radical mind shift in your definition of success. One of the greatest reasons you fail, quit, or never even get started, is because you have improperly defined success. This definition then leads to frustration when your life does not meet these unrealistic expectations.

Living someone else's definition of success can be frustrating to anyone, but this frustration is amplified when you live with a limitation. You cannot look at someone else who is a healthy type A personality and moves like a chipmunk jacked up on excessive amounts of caffeine, and try to mimic their path. You will never be able to achieve their success because you are not them and never will be. And that is awesome.

You must forgo this preconceived idea of normal. You are you, and you can be the best you there has ever been. If you define success properly within the framework of your own limitations, you can be an extremely successful Raging Sloth.

WARPED DEFINITION OF SUCCESS

The definition of success on dictionary.com is: "the favorable or prosperous termination of attempts or endeavors; *the accomplishment of one's goals.*" The last part is crucial in that you are achieving your own brand of success. Success is simply defining your goals and then executing them.

You may have goals to start your own business, spend more time with your family, make a certain amount of money, be able to challenge and help people, start a nonprofit organization, or serve others with a specific need. Success is realized when you are specific in WHAT you want to achieve and HOW you are going to achieve your defined goals.

Dr. Linda Seger wrote, "Americans tend to define success by money, and by what money can buy. We are known around the world as a rather materialistic country, always striving after things and defining success by the accoutrements that money can buy – such as our snazzy cars, the size of our homes and designer clothes. And that's just what we get – more things. This doesn't mean more fulfillment or contributing to make the world better in some way. It simply means more things."

We can't define success solely based upon what we can accumulate. Success is problematic in our society and it is time we changed the definition. You can search the web and find a thousand different people giving you a thousand different ways to achieve success as long as you follow their proven formula, which works great if you are just like them.

Don't get me wrong—I have listened to, learned from, and followed many of these people, and most of them have been very useful in providing effective tools for my own success.

But if I define my success on their terms, I would be constantly frustrated. A simple task for them can be an extremely difficult endeavor for me. I have to digest their advice with caution against my own abilities and limitations.

There is also the issue of being lured into an idea of success through social media, news, and reality television by viewing "successful" people—who in reality are no more successful than you, but have just created an avenue to get your attention.

Courtney Spritzer and Stephanie Abrams, when discussing this illusion, stated: "When businesses, celebrities and the neighbor down the street are all in a competitive fight for internet attention, it's tough to separate the truly popular from the seriously 'followed.' While social media can be a blessing for many companies when it comes to online branding and marketing, it can bring the curse of inauthenticity."

We need to be wary of other people's definition of success—because if we jump full force into trying to live someone else's life, we are usually in for a long and painful fall.

RECONCILING SUCCESS

My life was on the verge of imploding because of my skewed definition of success. It was a cruel reality to awaken and not recognize my life in my pursuit of other people's goals. While watching from a distance, I believed that if I could attain the house they lived in, the clothes they wore, and the job they had, I would be successful in spite of my pain. It was ironic how much time and energy I was exerting to prove something to people who did not care.

Even once I had attained all this stuff, I was miserable and hollow inside. I had a great job, a nice house, new cars, and fancy clothes. But I was out of sorts. I knew I had attained a reality where I could not keep up the pace. I physically could not keep up the pace to live a lifestyle I did not even want. I was left empty by pursuing a path that was not life-giving to my soul. By defining success using someone else's standards, I felt like a failure because I could not keep going at their pace, speed, and drive.

This sudden awakening made me take a step back and evaluate what really mattered in my life. How do I, or how can I, define success not only for myself and what I want to achieve, but how can I define it within the limitations of my own life, pain, and physical restrictions? By defining success on my own terms, I broadened my perspective and expectations to be able to live a more fulfilled life.

One of my major priorities is my family. They are important to me, and making myself available to my wife and kids is a major influence in what decisions I make. With my family being a high priority, my career needed to create ample space for them.

I needed to mark out a career based upon what I wanted to achieve and accomplish, and ultimately to get the kind of life I wanted which, if you remember, is my definition of success. I no longer needed to look to anyone else for validation of my success.

The gradual shift in discovering a new definition of success started with a simple idea to write a book, not specifically this book. I wanted to write a book because it was one of those dreams I had buried deep in my soul, long forgotten since I graduated college and ventured into the corporate world.

I was always writing. I journaled almost every day, writing blog posts even though I had no website, and I'd written extensively in past jobs. I also discovered that even in my deepest pain, I could lose myself in writing. If I got into a "zone" during a writing session, the pain would be put on the back burner and I could lose myself in the story for a brief period. Writing had become very therapeutic for me.

But if I was going to write a book, I wanted to write a *great* book, not a good book. I wanted to set myself up for the best possible chance of success. Having spent many years consulting and in full-time ministry, I knew God had blessed me with the tools and talents to achieve certain goals. I had been given great training and a foundation I could use to achieve success.

But I had never written a book before, so this process was far outside my comfort zone. To be better prepared, I began doing research on how to start my own company, network, build a platform, build a tribe, write a book, build an email list, and so on. I was fully immersed in figuring out the proper steps needed to best ensure my success during this process.

But there was a problem. While I was immersing myself in all these content-specific gurus, I was noticing a pattern.

Almost all of the videos I watched, webinars I signed up for, conferences I attended, and training I went through, were created by highly caffeinated type A juggernauts who ran at 100 mph and seemed to never sleep.

All these gurus talked about how they woke up first thing in the morning to wrestle a bear to the ground because it was refreshing. Then they would run a marathon to get the blood flowing. Once they completed their run, they would go launch a product and make $100,000 by 10 a.m. Then it was off to the gym for a mid-morning workout.

On the way home from the gym, they would start another company while stuck in traffic. In the middle of all these activities, they were tweeting, posting on Facebook, and sending out e-mail updates while running their board meetings. And don't forget, they spent their evenings at the homeless shelter handing out soup because they had a big heart. All the while, they were constantly saying they were just an average individual like me.

They were not like me, not by a long shot. They had so much energy exuding through their presentations I had to take a nap after watching their presentations. How could I ever keep up?

I eventually got frustrated and a little depressed. I could never keep up with this level of energy. I would love to have this type of energy. To be able to drive through a day with so much vibrancy and productivity, never being distracted by pain, discomfort, or a complete lack of concentration.

For me to be successful, I have to be realistic with my limitations—which is why engaging my limitation was the first step. I cannot keep up with the cheetahs. If I follow their definition of success as the only way to succeed with my own career, then I'm at a loss as to how I can succeed.

Once I got over the initial shock and depression, I started thinking there had to be another way. There had to be some type of training or plan for the rest of us sloths who are dealing with uninvited obstacles and challenges but still want to be successful and do something impactful. The problem was I could not find any helpful resources.

At certain times in my life, I had been successful in the business world and with a full-time ministry, but I knew I could have accomplished far more had I been given the right direction or guidance. In both instances, I hit a wall because of my pain. I was attempting to model success after other individuals because this was all I knew.

Eventually, in both circumstances the pain or discomfort became too much to balance. I could never reconcile my pain with a regular full-time corporate job while attempting to meet the expectations of people in business or ministry.

I knew I had the ability to maneuver successfully around my own limitation to do something greater, but I really needed to be able to look at life, work, and relationships from a different view. The problem was I could never find a book or guide from someone in my situation that could get me on the right path.

On success, author and business leader Michael Hyatt stated: "Success has many determining factors, including dumb luck. But I've been thinking of one lately that's largely indispensable and totally learnable—persistence."

While I was running low on dumb luck, I did have persistence. This trait has not been optional in my life in dealing with my pain, and would become the greatest asset in turning my life upside down. I would dare to suggest persistence is probably one of your greatest assets, too.

I started putting together a specific plan. A manifesto to myself about how I could be successful, but it had to be on my terms.

This is how *The Raging Sloth* began, as a way to look at life a little differently, be successful on my terms, and learn to be successful not in spite of my limitation but by engaging my limitation. It helped me to accept what I was given, learn from my pain, and use it to my advantage in becoming the individual I knew was inside me.

ENGAGING SUCCESS

To begin this process, I had to start changing my perspective, look at life a little differently, and be more positive with my limitation to create a space for success to happen.

If I kept on living my past life, I would make myself, my wife, my kids, and everyone around me miserable, if I hadn't already. I was living a life in someone else's shoes, trying to be someone I neither wanted to be nor wanted to become.

Leadership guru and author John Maxwell said, "When it comes to change, there are three seasons of timing: People change when they hurt enough that they have to, when they learn enough that they want to, and when they receive enough that they are able to." I was at a strange place where all three of these seasons were intersecting at once.

A drastic, cataclysmic change needed to occur in my life or I would continue to live a life of regrets. I would never know what I was capable of completing or accomplishing because I was letting my limitation define and restrict me from truly living an abundant life.

But it was going to take a lot of introspection—to be honest with myself and create a realistic plan that would define success on my terms and no one else's. I had to stop dreaming about the change and put the plan into action.

This is why you need to continue on with your plan and sit down to define success for yourself. Is success spending more time with your family, making more money, having more free time, living in a certain place, or doing a certain job? What does success look like to you and how will you specifically achieve those goals?

Your plan will be specific and timely and give you the steps you need to achieve your goals. Like with any plan, you will also have to be flexible with these goals so you can make adjustments to your own limitations and the many variables life throws your way.

Getting to a point of transforming my idea of success was not an easy transition. I had to unlearn many ideas, traditions, and practices I had engaged in for many years and believed as truth. They were true for someone who was whole, but not for me.

Beginning the process felt like I was wading through thigh-high mud. It was slow, painful, and tedious. But the more I kept at it, the more I trudged through the mire, the easier the process became. My mind began to open and the pathway became clear.

UPSIDE-DOWN LIFE PROPOSITION

I researched many different avenues of success and what it may look like. While there may be many different paths, the following process is what I created to redefine success within the boundaries of my limitation. You can download your free Raging Sloth Companion Guide at: www.theragingsloth.com/bonus.

The first step I took was to create a mission statement for my life, which I call the Upside-Down Life Proposition. In basic terms, this is the "What do I want out of life?" question. Specifically, what does your life look like when you choose to live upside-down?

What do I want to do with my life? What do I want others to see in my life? How do I want to help others? This is the overall goal in which I will define success. Everything I do will revolve around this mission statement.

My personal Upside-Down Life Proposition is to "create a better adventure in order to live life upside-down." This proposition guides my personal goals, my company, and my work. It is also the foundation of how I relate to my wife, kids, and other relationships, and of what I want to offer to others.

I want to be there for my wife and kids to help them live a better adventure. I want to make myself available as a spouse and father to guide them on their next great adventure. I also want this for others. I want to create a space for others who are suffering to grow, to realize life can be awesome in spite of our circumstances, and to create a better adventure while engaging their obstacles.

I write this mission statement down every day. It is a constant reminder to live life upside-down every day and never settle for right-side-up living.

OUTLINE GOALS

The next step I took after creating my proposition was to outline specific goals. What steps, tasks, or activities are going to help me live upside-down? If I want to create a better adventure in my own life and guide others to a better adventure, then what are the specific steps it will take to accomplish this scenario?

I began to write specific goals of writing a book, creating content, outlining coaching strategies, and building a website. Personally, I wanted intentional time with my wife and children. I created goals on growing personal and professional relationships.

I also needed to grow myself to get there, so I added goals of reading and studying my Bible, writing workshops, coaching training, website design, and leadership development. In order to grow my business, I had to grow myself, and I could not lose sight of moving both objectives along at the same time.

Like all goals, these need to be SMART goals: Specific, Measurable, Attainable, Realistic, and Timely. For my limitation, I needed to make sure I was acutely aware of the last three attributes.

I needed to make sure my goals were attainable, that they were realistic with my limitation, and that I could reach them in a timely fashion. When creating my goals, I needed to be realistic or I would immediately insert frustration into my plan, which I needed to avoid.

I knew I would fail in different aspects and I could allow for those missteps. But I needed to set myself up for success as much as possible. If I was unrealistic in my attempts, then I would sabotage my success before I could even start, and this was a pitfall I needed to avoid. It was important to insert my limitation into my goals to avoid frustration, guilt, or excuses.

OUTLINE LIMITATION

The next step you need to take is to effectively and honestly outline your limitation. For this exercise, I spend time outlining the pain I experience on any given day, how it affects me through the course of the day, and if there are breaks I can take to counter the pain.

For example, if I wake up in moderate pain, am I able to work through the pain? If so, are their external issues I need to deal with, like standing up more during the day, taking a walk, or working from a recliner?

To determine any internal issues, I ask myself the following questions: How is the pain affecting my attitude? Can I still think clearly today? Can I handle the workload I created for the day? Is there any type of situation I may need to avoid with other people because of the impact pain has on me?

If the pain is more severe, what is a better course of action for the day? Do I need to take a nap, rest more, or move activities to another day where I can be more effective? What activities can I work on today?

I have noticed that on days when the pain is more intense, I can do more of what I call "input" activities, or internal-growth activities. While it is more difficult to deal with people, act chipper, or even produce any type of content on high-pain days, it is easier to watch training videos, read, align my calendar, or attend online webinars. These are the inputs I draw upon for internal growth.

To look at my limitation from an integrated standpoint, I have to catalogue my pain and how it affects me at different times, and what my best response should be in each instance. This is the realistic part of my goal-setting process.

This exercise forces me to stop trying to work around my pain and face it head-on. Being honest about the daily distractions of my pain allows me to effectively and more efficiently work with my pain to be more productive.

I've become more realistic with my schedule and what I can accomplish than ever before. Being realistic lets me be flexible with my tasks, adjust my schedule as necessary, and set attainable expectations. I keep my dreams and goals set high; I just change the pathway to how I will reach them.

EXECUTE AGAINST GOALS

Once I had defined my goals and limitations, the next step was to write an executable plan to achieve those goals. I did this by taking my yearly goals and breaking them down into monthly and daily tasks. Each month, I would write what major tasks needed to happen in order to achieve my goals in that particular time period.

I accomplished this process by being specific and realistic. If I am writing a book, then I am outlining which chapters need to be completed that month. In order to be more intentional with my wife and children, I write down what date nights look like with my wife or when breakfast with my children will occur. If I plan on reading so many books over the course of the year, I have to be specific and write down which books I am going to read that month.

By breaking my goals down month by month, I allow myself to revisit my goals routinely and see if I'm on track or if I need to make adjustments.

I've learned to be specific and realistic with what I need to accomplish each month, and decide whether I need to adjust and push something onto the next month because of my limitation. This process allows me to keep my goals and limitations in a more realistic balance.

Next, I created a daily plan. I would sit down either the night before or early in the morning and outline what I need to specifically accomplish each day to stay on track for my goals.

This task may seem tedious to you, and trust me, I hated daily plans. I never imagined myself completing daily plans. But what I realized was I hated them because they were a constant source of frustration. If I wrote down tasks I couldn't complete because of my pain, and if I didn't allow for any adjustments, it was a recipe for frustration.

But once I started the process of inserting my limitation into my daily plan, it was freeing to be able to work through the day allowing for the obstacle, instead of being sidetracked by the obstacle. The simple step of making space for my pain helped me to be more productive.

ALLOW SPACE FOR LIMITATION

Allowing space for your limitation is probably the most important aspect of your plan and your definition of success.

The reality for someone living with an obstacle is that it may be consistent or it may be completely random.

Either way, it affects how you work, how you live, and what you accomplish. You do not gain anything by ignoring its effects on your life. Instead, I want you to hit it head-on and address how it might affect your day, before it happens, so you can make a better decision if it does decide to derail you.

I will talk more about being flexible in a later chapter, but what I write down in my daily plan are my Flex Points. How I can be flexible today because of my limitation? This is essentially your "reward" area. How are you going to be good to yourself today so you do not get too enveloped by your limitation or get sidetracked? You may reward yourself with a movie, social media time, a walk, a treat, or a nap.

The goal of flexing is to allow yourself a reward that will take you away from your obstacle, make you more effective, and allow you to return back to your work in the same day to complete your tasks. By using this space on a daily basis, you are learning to give yourself grace during difficult circumstances.

I use this space because I struggle with sitting for long periods of time due to my hip. Unfortunately, I don't do much better with standing because of nerve damage in my foot. For me, the best use of my time is to work a segmented day.

I am generally up early and get a couple of hours of work completed. I then eat breakfast, shower, and get dressed. I work for a couple of hours more before stopping to do my daily physical therapy. The exercises wake me back up and keep my body from getting stiff from the sitting.

I eat lunch and then continue to work for a few more hours. At this point, I usually need to take an extended break. I will enjoy a walk or a bike ride if I'm feeling up to it. On more trying days I may just nap or grab a coffee with a friend.

This "flexing" keeps my body from getting in knots sitting for a while, but it also allows me to clear my head so I can come back to my work more refreshed and capable of completing my tasks. I have learned that the worst case scenario for me both physically and mentally is sitting at a desk all day staring at my computer.

The next space you need to define on a daily basis is a Break Point. What if your limitation becomes too overbearing during the course of the day to complete your normal tasks? How can you give yourself a break?

You absolutely need to fill this out every day to alleviate guilt or frustration in your life. I fill this space out in the morning based on how I feel when I get up. In this space, you need to either define alternate activities you can accomplish if the distraction is too great or check out altogether.

Most days I can work through my pain. But there are days I struggle to complete my outlined tasks because the pain is draining too much of my energy and I cannot think clearly. On these days, I outline the input tasks I can do: read a book, complete more online training, watch videos of content I am attempting to learn, organize my notes, or just listen to a podcast.

These activities do not require much of me but are still aligned with my goals, and most importantly, I feel like I am still being productive. By making it a habit to write the Break Points down, I am creating space for my limitation within my schedule. This process eliminates the guilt and frustration I would place upon myself when I did not feel like I could complete an activity.

On really bad days, when it is difficult to finish a task or even read, I give myself the grace to check out. This may mean just a simple nap. I put everything on hold, lie down, and see if I can recover and come back to my tasks.

Taking a break does work at times, but there are days when I cannot recover and I need to put everything on hold and move it to the next day. My body and mind are too far gone to do anything productive.

By writing down Break Points and making it a part of my plan, I am eliminating the frustration and guilt of not being able to accomplish what I think I should be completing on any given day. I am executing against goals in a realistic fashion because I am incorporating my obstacle into my plan.

YOUR DEFINITION OF SUCCESS

I tell my children being comfortable in their own skin is one of the greatest gifts they can give themselves. The same is true in defining success. If you can come to a good working definition of success in your own life, then you are living in your own skin and no one else's— which means you do not have to compare yourself to anyone else. You don't have to be frustrated because you have not achieved someone else's dream.

Stop trying to "fit in" or wish you could feel "normal." The upside-down life is the new normal, and there are literally millions of people out there who are in a similar situation and are normal just like you. Grab hold of your life and choose to live it upside-down.

You are an awesome you, and you can become the best you on the face of this earth. Now you have a specific plan to achieve your goals. Defining success for yourself to achieve your goals is how you become an unstoppable Raging Sloth.

6

STEP THREE:
KNOWING YOUR PASSIONS

The Pitfalls and Promises
Behind Your Passions

We don't read and write poetry because it's cute.
We read and write poetry because we are members
of the human race. And the human race is filled with
passion. And medicine, law, business, engineering,
these are noble pursuits and necessary to sustain life.
But poetry, beauty, romance, love, these are what we
stay alive for. ~ John Keating, Dead Poets Society

We all know someone who is a little too passionate about a subject. I mean, enthusiastically impassioned by the most mundane activity. They are the type of person you admire for their passion, but you do not necessarily want to be near them in their moments of exuberance.

You know that one friend who loves sports maybe just a little too much? I can't say I am really passionate about football, but I may get a little too involved when watching my favorite college or NFL team play. This became apparent to me a few years ago when I realized my dog would leave the room whenever I was watching a football game. Evidently, she was not a fan of my exuberant displays for the home team.

I see this type of passion in my sister Tammy when it comes to art. While I can appreciate art as much as any individual who struggles to draw stick figures, the passion my sister has when it comes to viewing paintings is admirable.

I experienced this passion firsthand many years ago when we went to the National Gallery of Art in Washington, DC. Walking through the museum, I could appreciate the colors, the light, and even the minute detail artists would endeavor to create when painting the human face, for instance, like Van Gogh, or with fruit, like Cezanne. I was amazed at the mountains by Bierstadt, or scenery by Monet. Again, I have zero ability to draw, so even the welcome sign in the foyer was impressive to me.

But as my sister viewed these paintings, I could tell she was seeing something far deeper than I could comprehend. I would look at a painting and state, "That's nice!" My sister would stand there for what seemed an eternity and scan every millimeter of the painting in awe of what the artist had created. I knew the depths of what she was experiencing would be eternally lost on me, but I completely admired her passion, and because of her I have a greater appreciation for art.

IMPORTANCE OF PASSION

Passion is important in your life. It is extremely important in your relationships, but it is also necessary when it comes to what inspires your soul, what you want out of life, and how you want to be successful.

You understand this truth because you have been misguided or have taken the wrong path due to your misinterpretation of your passions. When you don't understand your passions, then you begin to make poor decisions that lead to false journeys. You may also misinterpret your passions and become frustrated when life, or your career, does not work out the way you planned.

This misguided passion unfolded on the big screen in the movie *Jerry Maguire* with Tom Cruise in the role of the main character. Jerry works for a high-powered sports management firm whose bottom line is all about money. One evening, Jerry has an epiphany and stays up all night writing his mission statement for the future of the company. He was passionate, he was coming alive, and he felt rejuvenated.

What started out as a one-page document quickly became twenty-five. You can see tears in his eyes as all the memories, thoughts, and ideas he had as a young sports agent burst through after having been buried for years in the process of building the firm's reputation.

In his passionate fury, he races to the nearest copy store and prints 110 copies with a nice simple cover that rivaled *The Catcher in the Rye*. He brilliantly entitled his manifesto "The Things We Think and Do Not Say."

He enters work the next day to cheers and applause from his coworkers for finally saying what they all had been thinking and desperately wanted to say themselves. But upon entering his boss's office, Jerry is abruptly fired for writing such an insane literary proposition.

Our passions can drive us to unlimited heights, but if we do not fully understand how to categorize them effectively, we too could end up like Jerry Maguire—full of passion, but with no place to fulfill our passion.

EVALUATING PASSION

There are two basic reasons we need to evaluate our passions thoroughly and appropriately. These reasons are two sides to the same coin, but both need to be held in balance and held in check in order to be successful so we do not stay up all night writing a mission statement that gets us fired.

The first side of the coin is the more obvious. We need to see what makes us tick, what brings us alive—like my sister with art. What could we wake up every morning doing and not even care if we get paid for doing it? It is important, very important, that we find out what makes us tick, what we love to do at the depths of our soul.

I have always enjoyed teaching, speaking, and writing. To put a presentation together, complete the research, shape it into a compelling story, and successfully deliver it from a stage has always brought life to my soul. That is the type of passion I would follow even if no one paid me.

I also found a passion in writing (which was very odd for me since I was the kid in school who got his paper back with more red ink on it than the black ink I had originally penned). Writing was also a surprise passion because my complete lack of understanding around grammar and the English language.

I found writing late in life and really did not see it as a passion. We all have to write for one reason or another, and I had lumped this activity into all of the other "must dos" of life. But I have journaled since high school and held several jobs that allowed me to write.

The writing was a by-product of the public speaking I enjoyed because I usually wrote out in entirety what I was going to say. This always allowed me to file through my notes for particular content later.

In the process, I completely overlooked the joy I found in writing. I remember how excited I was when I had an article published in a local newsletter. I should have paid more attention to my response. I cut the article out, framed it, and hung it on my office wall. I was very proud. But the inner demons were screaming too loudly in my head, "You are not good enough!" for me to fully rationalize this passion.

I don't usually get up early for much, but when I began to awaken this part of my soul, I also began to awaken at 5 a.m. every day to write. I was writing about all types of topics. In the beginning, I really didn't know what I was going to do with this content. But I kept on writing, writing, and writing.

Slowly, I noticed that even in those bad days when the pain was pretty intense, I could lose myself for an hour or two in the writing process, not even realizing how much time had passed or how long I had sat in front of the computer typing. It was as if someone was slowly pulling the curtain back on a reality I never knew existed.

UNDERSTANDING PASSION

This side of your passion is necessary to understand because if you have gone through a cataclysmic moment in your life through pain, suffering, challenges, or problems, you probably do not look at life the same way as everyone else. The pursuits of money, fame, or traditional success will not seem important. They will in fact look like baneful, lifeless pursuits because the traditional path of achieving corporate success comes up short and lacking.

When an obstacle is placed directly in your path and your life is turned upside down, chances are the experience probably makes you a little more altruistic than the average individual. You may want to help others, or be in some profession or non-profit where you are aiding and assisting others. When you live with an obstacle, having the ability to give back or help others can be a tremendous driving force in living your passion.

This passion is what gets you out of bed in the mornings when your body does not want to cooperate. Having a passion that entices you to get up and engage the day can make a tremendous difference in how you live life and move toward success.

This is part of living life on your terms. You need to be able to pour your heart and soul into whatever project you desire. Life is challenging, and every day is an obstacle.

Being able to invest yourself in a passion or something greater can allow you to come alive regardless of your circumstances. But it will be up to you to find what's in your heart and see how it can manifest itself into a viable reality.

The flipside of this coin is understanding the part of your passion you should not pursue, which is just as important as knowing a passion to pursue. You may be passionate about a hobby, a talent, or a theme in your life, but you need to keep it only as an enjoyable pastime.

Just because you are passionate about watching football or singing in the shower does not mean you can drop everything and go pro in these areas. The outcome would be disastrous and possibly very painful.

Watch an early-season episode of *American Idol* and you'll see individuals who should have kept their singing as an exercise they only engaged in during an evening of karaoke. Even though they are passionate about singing, they are either not very good, were lied to their entire life, or did not spend the time honing their craft to be successful in their passion. *American Idol* is a great example of misplaced passion and how it can backfire. But that is why it makes for great reality television.

I thoroughly enjoy music. I play guitar and bass, and I love playing music as much as listening to it. I will rarely pass up an opportunity to play somewhere. If you are ever in the car with me, you might have to suffer through listening to me sing along with whatever song is currently playing.

Even though I am passionate about music, it would be absolutely foolish for me to pursue music as a profession. I came to the conclusion many years ago that this was simply a hobby and not a professional pursuit. By placing it in this category, I began to enjoy playing more because it took the pressure off of trying to pursue a hobby as a career.

If you are able to look at your life and categorize your passions as either pursuits or hobbies, it can help you begin the journey of finding your habitat—the environment where you are most comfortable and where you can thrive upside-down.

IDENTIFYING PASSION

You can take four different viewpoints or steps to properly categorize your pursuits. You can begin this process by using the Passion Assessment in the Companion Guide at www.theragingsloth.com/bonus. Write down your passions on a piece of paper, or if you are more of a geek, you can create a complicated spreadsheet on your computer. No matter what method you use, you need to begin the process of outlining your passions.

STEP1: FREE TIME

The first way to identify a passion is to simply see what you do in your free time. Check your calendar and see what you fill your time with that does not have to do with work. On weekends, weeknights, holidays, or vacations, what do you enjoy doing?

What will you participate in at the expense of time with your friends or family? What does this activity entail and how do you participate? Find those passions in your life you just enjoy participating in regardless of the timing or who has joined in the activity. Rate these activities and your willingness to participate in them on a scale from 1-10.

STEP 2: FRIENDS

The second step is to simply ask your friends what they think you are passionate about. You might be surprised at what you hear, and this is a good lesson in understanding what passions you might have overlooked.

When I began to write, I only told my close friends what I was doing. I was still very uncomfortable with the title "author" and didn't really want to let anyone know what I was attempting to pursue. This way, I did not have to fully commit to the process and could drop the project the first time I got frustrated.

But to my surprise, every one of them—let me repeat: every single friend—said, "I'm not surprised. I could always see you writing." They may not have been surprised, but I was floored. This was not something I had seen in myself at all, but my close friends saw this characteristic in me.

I also finally realized why my wife had been trying to get me to go to all of these writing conferences for years. It was truly an amazing affirmation of where I was headed and that I was on the right track. It was also incredible motivation to finish the project. Do not underestimate using what loved ones see in you as you pursue your passion.

STEP 3: SKILLS/INVENTORY TEST

A third way to identify a passion is to take one of the many skills/inventory tests you can find on the Internet. These can be somewhat sterile and you have to take them with a grain of salt, but they can at least give you the "you are here" part of the map. Giving you a basic idea of where you are located can help point you in a general direction. (You can find more skills/inventory resources in the Companion Guide.)

These tests can also be a guide in discerning between your talents and your passions. When you have looked at what you enjoy but also what you are good at doing, do the two subjects align? How can you use the similarity or disparity to include in your plan to live life on your terms? This is how you can use these inventory tests effectively.

STEP 4: EXCITEMENT

The last way to discover your passion is to simply take what you have learned from the first three steps and find out what gets you excited. What gets you to wake up in the morning and is something you wouldn't mind doing in your free time without pay?

This should be the easiest step as you simply need to review your life, or what your friends have told you, and figure out what gets you going, what makes you happy, what you would quit your job in a second to go do (although I don't suggest this just yet). Figure out what lights a fire underneath you as you begin to build your path toward success.

The flipside of this exercise is to understand what drains you. Is it being around people, sticking to someone else's schedule, public speaking, or talking to strangers? We will discuss entering your danger zones in a later chapter in more detail, but it is important to understand the balance between what you enjoy that gives you life and what drains you.

For example, if you are a phenomenal singer with the voice of an angel but are deathly afraid of being in front of other people, then this is necessary information for you to know how to live upside-down.

You will eventually have to make the decision of whether you can overcome your fear of getting in front of other people or should move on to another passion. But you need to understand how both parts fit into your life.

After you have identified your passions, you need to identify whether each passion is one to pursue as a career or to pursue as a hobby. Now, it is time to take an honest assessment of what you have learned and try to figure out what needs to stay a hobby and what you think you can make a run at, tweak, or turn into a business. This is the first step, so don't try to run too far ahead. All we are attempting to accomplish here is to figure out what makes us tick and what gets our engines going.

If you can start with your passion, then you can begin the path of being able to live your own adventure on your terms, and with a greater understanding of your limitations. It is important to take this step; otherwise, you end up continuing your false journey, or begin one. You could be pursuing a passion that should only be relegated to a hobby. Or, a misguided one that could take you down the wrong road.

In transforming into a Raging Sloth, you must not only understand your own passion, but also be able to live within this passion in everything you accomplish.

7

STEP FOUR: ADJUSTING YOUR HABITAT

Finding Your Way Back Home

The ache for home lives in all of us, the safe place where we can go as we are and not be questioned.
~ Maya Angelou

Leith and Aaron met in college, fell quickly for one another, and were married shortly after graduation. They began their lives together by moving to Colorado, getting their careers on track, and welcoming the birth of their son.

Life was good and everything seemed on track as their dreams were unfolding as planned. They had moved into their brand-new house and welcomed their new daughter, a beautiful baby girl named Hadley, a few days later. But in Aaron's words "their perfect world would change."

They knew something was not quite right when Hadley was born, but no one could identify it clearly. At four months old, Leith and Aaron would soon find out Hadley was born with only part of her brain and the rest of her brain was underdeveloped. She had the basic functions to keep her body alive, but would require round-the-clock care for the rest of her life.

Leith and Aaron's habitat was about to turn upside down. The life they had been living was gone and it would never return. The shock, fear, and disbelief of the unknowns facing Hadley and their future were overwhelming. A life of meaning became a life of survival. Leith put her school and career on hold to care for Hadley. Aaron was learning how to navigate leading a family he had no foundation or blueprint to comprehend.

If you asked them, they would not have changed anything, but the life they were going to live was unexpected and would require them to discover how to live differently. They would have to live life upside-down and seek out a new way of living in a very different habitat.

A SLOTH'S HABITAT

Have you ever felt like a fish out of water, like you knew beyond a shadow of a doubt you were out of place? A few years ago on a trip in the Colca Canyon mountains of Peru, I had this feeling. We were traveling through these small villages in the canyon and would hold a worship service at night, along with speaking and crafts for the kids. This all sounds very benign and likely what you would expect from your average white guy on a mission trip in South America.

But to put the scene in perspective, I am about six-foot-three and, as mentioned, very white. The mountain towns we visited were inhabited by the original Quechua Indian people. The average height of the men and women in the villages was around five feet.

These towns were also very small and had few to no automobiles and little electricity or running water. So when I showed up and walked through the town square, children would run up behind me shouting, *"Gigante, gigante!"* referring to me as "the giant."

To make matters worse, I am not very well versed in the metric system—blame it on my rural Texas education. When the children in the towns asked me, in Spanish and meters, how tall I was, I might have inadvertently told them I was nine feet tall.

If you are ever in the Andes mountains of Peru and hear a story about the *"gigante blanco,"* that would be me. Although I was very welcomed and the people were extremely gracious, I felt out of place.

We generally feel out of place when we are not working or functioning in our natural habitat. One of the unique characteristics of sloths is they spend their entire lives in trees. Trees are their natural habitat and where they thrive most.

Sloths prefer the tops of trees covered with wooded vines to provide protection from predators and shelter from sun during the day. Trees also provide body support for their much needed naps.

The sloth is indigenous to the jungles of Central and South America, with the general opinion being that the sloth cannot survive outside of this specific habitat. In fact, the maned three-toed sloth has only been able to survive a few months in captivity. Whether the sloth is tied to the habitat or the habitat cannot be reproduced, it cannot survive outside its natural surroundings.

Living in the trees is essential for the sloth's existence. When a sloth's habitat is destroyed through natural disaster or deforestation, they will die if not moved to another habitat. It usually entails human intervention to transport them to a new home. They would be too exposed if they stay in the same habitat that, unfortunately, no longer had trees.

Trees are where a sloth belongs. This is where they are fed, where they sleep, and where they are safe. Many of you would do well to be keenly aware of the environment where you can thrive, especially when you are not working, or sometimes even living, in your own habitat or in the right habitat.

In some cases, you have strayed so far from the trees you no longer recognize your own habitat, and yet you can't identify the feeling that you're in the wrong place and are not safe. You are dying on the inside but cannot say why, nor do you understand how to reverse course.

OBSERVING YOUR HABITAT

Everyone creates their own habitat, whether right or wrong, once they begin to leave home and venture out on their own. You create your habitat based on your own and other people's expectations, dreams, traditions, or ideas.

This habitat can be the expectation of your parents who wanted you to be a doctor, lawyer, or college professor. The habitat could even be the dreams of a boyfriend or girlfriend who thinks it would be awesome if you stayed in the band.

Your expectation could be from a spouse who wants you to maintain a steady job to support the family, or even your own expectations or ideas of success. Maybe you think it would be cool to show up to work every day in a zipped hoodie and t-shirt like Mark Zuckerberg at Facebook.

No matter the source of the expectation, over time you have worked hard enough to establish a life meeting this goal. At the very least, you have created a comfortable existence in your attempt to balance life and work.

Even though this habitat may not have been your dream, you are comfortable here and can make a living—except when an obstacle is placed in front of you. Without the ability to overcome your obstacle, your current habitat is getting more and more suffocating. Your obstacle magnifies and becomes like a megaphone shouting in your ear all you have missed and all that is wrong in your current world.

You make up excuses for why this habitat is right for you: you have a good job, you have a family to support, you are too old, or you are in too much pain or suffering to make a change.

You can even intellectually argue you are in the right habitat because you are being responsible and providing for your family, which is a noble cause. But you are dying inside because you have a deep longing in your heart for a habitat more conducive to your limitation.

LIVING IN THE WRONG HABITAT

I spent many years working at the wrong job, far from my habitat, and it was breaking me apart. There was nothing wrong with the companies I worked for. Some of the people I worked with are phenomenal individuals for whom I have the utmost respect. I was very honored to have the opportunity to work with them. But I was not working in the right space because of my limitation. Part of my issue is that I have no control over my pain, and being under someone else's authority in different aspects of my career was extremely challenging.

To compound the issue, my job required me to travel to client sites all over the US and England. A five-hour flight spent writhing in pain was not fun by any stretch of the imagination.

Plus, I would have days when my entire concentration was on suppressing the pain, which left little energy to go above and beyond on a project, let alone meet the status quo. Looking back, I realized I was doing the minimum possible in an attempt to balance my pain and work.

I was so far from my natural environment, so far from my habitat, I really did not know what to do or even know where to begin. I left my natural habitat thinking I could live right-side up and function like everyone else. But then the pain returned to remind me I could not live this way.

I had put myself in a far worse position. I was truly the sloth on the jungle floor waiting to be eaten by a predator because I did not realize how fully exposed I had made myself. But unlike the sloth, I did not know what to do. I had forgotten how to climb and get back up into the trees.

The realization that my pain would not go away, that it was a challenge I was going to have to live with, destroyed my habitat. I could not go back up into those trees even if I so desired because they were gone. There was nothing for me. I had to mourn the loss of my old habitat and then begin the process of finding not just a new habitat, but *my* new habitat.

This is why it's important to find your passion. If you are working with a limitation, then it is easier and better if you can work within your passion. The trials of the daily grind become less of a burden when you are working on what lights your soul on fire.

If you are living with pain or discomfort, it can be difficult to accomplish basic daily tasks. It's much easier to push the pain down and jump out of bed if you are excited and passionate about what you are doing that day.

Being able to work for myself, I put all of my energy into creating what I can when I am feeling good. This way, on bad days, I can allow myself rest and to recover without guilt. I have more control over my situation, and I am far more productive in this setting. The ability to feel more natural in my own habitat is astounding—especially when the alternative is working with a limitation and trying to live under someone else's requirements and expectations in their habitat.

CHANGING YOUR ADVENTURE

Realizing you need to change your habitat is one epiphany, but how do you begin the process of changing your adventure? In some cases, the answer may be seeing if there are ways to adjust your current job, especially if you do enjoy your work or have a great boss. Can your work be flexible in any way to best support your habitat?

Are there other jobs within your company that can support you in your habitat? Do you need to make a career change altogether? Or is running your own business from the passion rising from your soul your best option? You do not need to call up your boss just yet to quit; you still need to be intentional and responsible. What you are doing is putting a plan together that can get you into your own habitat.

Your main goal right now is to do research. How do your passions, definitions of success, and habitat all line up to put you where you want and need to be? What will this habitat look like in your own life, and who are the people you can call who have walked this road before you? Search the Internet, watch some webinars, find some courses, send some emails, talk to friends, and join a tribe.

The unfortunate side of living with a limitation is while people might be sympathetic, no one is going to go out of their way to help you find your habitat. This is your responsibility and yours alone. You have to own it. No one is going to hand your habitat to you on a silver platter.

If you can begin to get your definition of success, your passion, and your habitat lined up, then work can actually become more enjoyable. Your limitation will seem less of a burden because you are working in your habitat where you are comfortable. Within your own habitat, you will be able to do things you've never dreamed of and be far more productive than you've ever imagined possible.

The flipside of this coin is if you don't do anything, you will be living outside your habitat. Even though you know something is wrong, you won't take the necessary steps to get back to your habitat.

Life on the ground is a slow, inevitable death, for you are leaving yourself exposed to every predator out there. When you climb back up into the trees, you find your comfort again and can turn back upside-down to live the life of a Raging Sloth.

By giving yourself purpose, you are also dramatically altering your personal habitat. Relationships can become easier, and relating to people in general can become less burdensome. Remember, you are not only searching for success in a career, but you are attempting to add purpose to your life and create success in all parts of your life. Success is creating this perfect balance within your habitat.

It is time to change your adventure. Regardless of how you view your life now or think you are limited, your life was made and you were created for an amazing adventure. But it is up to you to find out where this adventure lies.

If you never take the time to discover your new habitat and embrace a better adventure, then you will just remain a sloth. But when you engage the fire within your heart and blaze a new trail into YOUR adventure, then you will transform into a Raging Sloth.

8

STEP FIVE:
THE FELLOWSHIP OF
THE RAGING SLOTH

Building Community For Your Journey

When we honestly ask ourselves which person in our lives means the most to us, we often find that it is those who, instead of giving advice, solutions, or cures, have chosen rather to share our pain and touch our wounds with a warm and tender hand. ~ Henri Nouwen

We were brave men!

Men who kissed their wives and hugged their children good-bye as they walked out the door to go on an epic adventure years in the making. We were about to embark on a legendary voyage down the Royal Gorge section of the Arkansas River in Colorado. A group of men with just their bravery, an oar, and a life jacket jetting down one of Colorado's most perilous rapids.

The morning was calm as we arrived at the floatable vessels that would carry us on our dangerous trek. We silently put on our wet suits—well, as silently as you can stuff your excess body weight into a small, tight, rubbery suit. We donned our life vests, grabbed our oars, and set out to conquer the mighty river.

We began the escapade with a calm and eerie quiet, the kind you only find in early mornings, the water appearing like shimmering glass. But soon we found ourselves being tossed about as the boat violently hit the rapids with a pounding force worthy of a ship in a violent storm. We were prevailing, we were conquering the rapids, our fearless guide leading six brave warriors within the confines of our rubbery warship.

But then the unexpected happened. The rapids became too daunting for us to bear. We were riding an angry bull violently bucking to remove us from its back.

In the middle of the rapids, I looked to the back corner of the boat where one of our fellow rafters, Doug, was sitting, only to realize there was no Doug. He had been catapulted from the boat in the midst of our battle with the river. Yet Doug magically landed on a rock in the middle of the river in a squatted position like a hero who descended from the skies.

We did not have time to worry about Doug though, because the rapids were getting worse. I turned my eyes past Doug's vacant seat and, to my horror, realized our guide had abandoned his post. He had been tossed out of the boat, swallowed up by the raging river.

Through the spray of water coming up from the river, I could barely make out the scene behind us of our guide being pulled from the river by one of the boats trailing behind. He was safe.

But we were not.

There were still more rapids ahead and they were showing little mercy. We were a man down with no guide, and no discernible leadership whatsoever in our craft. Upon this sudden realization, we banded together as only men can do to take the river down and not let it crush our spirits.

But again, we were men, which means all five of us started barking out very different orders in unison hoping to keep the boat moving forward and avoid being capsized. The term *frantic chaos* does little to describe the utter despair and desperation within our tiny inflatable frame.

By what I can only call the grace of God, we survived the rapids and settled into a stretch of smoother water. We retrieved Doug and got our guide back into the boat and continued on our adventure.

Our guide looked around the boat and complimented us on how we handled ourselves alone through the torrential currents of the river. We all nodded silently, with accompanying grunts in agreement with our guide, no one wanting to acknowledge the reality of the chaos in the boat.

What we realized during this day, which will live in infamy in our own minds, is that we do not have to be the most capable, the most coordinated, or even the most adventurous (I do believe I heard some screams from the men on the boat upon realizing that we had lost our guide).

What matters most is that we worked together for a common purpose, even though our efforts looked very different. This single initiative allowed us to accomplish our goal of keeping the boat upright, regardless of how disconnected we looked in the process.

FORMING A FELLOWSHIP

Sloths, by nature, are solitary animals, but they cannot live their entire lives in solitude. They have to come together to mate, to care for their young, and for safety, which means they need each other to survive in difficult times.

An important characteristic of becoming a Raging Sloth is to never go at it alone. If you do, you will fail. There are no two ways around this situation. In order to succeed, in order to live a life on your terms, you are going to have to find a fellowship, a group, or a community of people you can join, have accountability, and find support with. Without these key elements, your path to success will be sabotaged by your own isolation.

One of the larger hurdles for people living with a limitation blazing a pathway toward success is the mindset of accomplishing all your goals on your own. You think you do not need anyone, or you think no one will understand your plight, so you attempt to forge ahead in solitude.

While it is true many will not understand your circumstances, it does not mean they will not be able to help you succeed. Even those who do not understand what you are going through can still be there to support you in your endeavor.

You might also be thinking it's just easier to do it on your own. We have all been in these types of situations before, and they can work well in small projects, but not in major goals.

Like most people in chronic pain, I do not always have the patience to show another person how to accomplish a task. But I also do not have the energy or stamina to complete all the necessary tasks myself. I have to endure the process and engage with others or I won't be able to accomplish anything.

You will never be able to succeed in the entirety of your goals on your own. There are too many obstacles, too many unforeseen ventures, and too many X factors you have not been able to take into account to make it on your own. This is even more true if you do not have any control over when your limitation rears its ugly head.

This has been one of my biggest mistakes, even though I have constantly tried to seek out a fellowship. What keeps getting in my way is the idea that no one understands what I am going through. Because of this singular thought, I pushed people away. I would not invite them in and did not gather the necessary people around me to succeed. I needed a better definition of a viable fellowship.

A FELLOWSHIP DEFINED

There is a story of a man who cannot hide his limitations because he has no ability to hide at all. His whole life consists of living on a three-by-six mat. His entire body is paralyzed and he is completely reliant on everyone around him. He has to beg so people will give him money. Even when they give him money, he has to rely on someone else to use the money to get him food and provide him a drink.

With his bowl sitting out to collect money, someone could easily walk by and take everything he had. What would he be able to do? Nothing! He would have to sit there and watch as someone walked off with all that he possessed.

But there is something remarkable about this person on the mat. He has friends, not just people who know him or people who feel obligated to take care of him. He has honest-to-goodness friends who want only the best for him and will do whatever they can for him even though he has nothing tangible to give them back in return.

This willingness to help this man came to fruition one day when a teacher going by the name Jesus came to town. The paralytic man, who we will call Bob, has friends who say, "I bet if we take Bob to see Jesus, he could make him walk again" and "We have all heard the stories of incredible miracles from Jesus. He could give you your strength back."

Bob is overwhelmed. He does not know what to say. He has heard of this Jesus and has often wondered if Jesus could heal him. But there is no way for Bob to get to Jesus, until now. For the first time in Bob's life he has hope and an opportunity for a real transformation.

Bob's friends look down and say to him, "Well that settles it. Bob, we are coming by tomorrow at nine a.m. to pick you up." And for Bob they literally mean it; they have to pick him up.

They come and get Bob in the morning, but by the time they get to the house where Jesus is speaking at, they realize it is packed. It is standing room only on the inside, and people are crowding around the windows and doorways just to hear him.

Bob's friends hadn't planned on this. They never thought it would be this crowded. They were so excited about getting Bob to see Jesus they completely forgot about all of the simple logistics involved in getting Bob directly in front of Jesus.

Bob says, "It is all right, guys. You gave it your best shot. I really appreciate what you have tried to do, but let's just go back to my spot. There is still time for me to make some money before nightfall." They're probably feeling a little defeated and tired by this point.

But Bob has persistent friends. They don't give up that easy. They sit in a circle and try to figure out what they can do. After an extensive brainstorming session, the only feasible plan is to lower Bob down through the roof.

This is what Bob's fellowship does. They dig through the roof, grab some ropes, and lower Bob down directly in front of a man speaking to a crowded room—all because they want what is best for Bob.

This is the definition of a fellowship. Psychologist Urie Bron-fenbrenner describes community as "a group which possesses and implements an irrational commitment to the well-being of its members." When we start to make irrational decisions like tearing a hole in a roof, disrupting one of the greatest teachers of the day, and lowering your friend to this man's feet, all because it is the only way that your friend can be helped, this is a true fellowship.

Bob had a severe limitation, but he also had dreams and aspirations, none of which he could have attained on his own. With the help of his fellowship, Bob attained more than he ever could have imagined on his own.

MY FELLOWSHIP

For many years, whenever I read the story of the paralyzed man, I always saw myself as one of the men carrying the mat. I always convinced myself I was strong enough to carry the other person, until life changed and I realized I was the man on the mat and I needed to allow others to carry me. When I take a step back and look at my life, the reality is I had these people holding me up longer than I realized.

My wife Erica has been a source of support and inspiration through all my harebrained ideas even though she did not always know where they would lead. Erica has also been there every step of the way through every pain episode, surgery, recovery, meltdown, and physical therapy session.

She did not dream of pursuing this life; yet, she has stood by me regardless. She does not understand my pain and suffering, but I cannot imagine what she has had to endure watching the man she married suffer and manage pain.

She has been there for me, cheered for me, and helped me live my life upside down. She even encouraged me—though we may not have known where our next paycheck would come from—to move forward to pursue my dream and live life on my terms.

My good friend Glenn has always supported me and given me opportunities to grow and prosper. Glenn will readily admit he has no idea what I have to endure and cannot even imagine what my life is like. But it has never stopped him from being supportive, encouraging me and helping me when I needed it most, or even simply listening to me as I tried to figure out what my life would look like living in constant pain.

Matt, my college roommate, has stood strong beside me even though we do not talk regularly. Matt has always been a source of encouragement. Through the highs and lows of life, Matt is the only person who asks how I am doing on a deeper level. *Was my soul all right.*

When we discussed how I was taking this little turn in my life to live it upside-down, even though I had no idea what it meant at that time, he was there for me. He would text me and ask how it was going, and he would offer encouragement, inspiration, or a prayer. Some days, whether he knew it or not, it was the little extra push I needed to stay on track, keep focused, and keep going.

Steve has been a tremendous support and a source of consistency throughout the last ten years. He is a retired Air Force F-16 pilot and goes 100 mph accomplishing more than I could ever dream. But he has always slowed down enough to provide focus and purpose in my life during those times when I needed it most.

Steve has always been a cheerleader in my life, even at times when I did not think I had much to cheer about. He is the type of friend we would all do well to have in our lives.

Scott, who I have known for years and who suffers from a similar problem, is the only person I know who truly understands my limitations—how I cannot always participate in an activity, how pain will slow me down, and how overwhelming and frustrating even the simplest of tasks can seem.

To have someone to share this burden with me is immeasurable. We all want to know we are not alone, no matter the situation or circumstance, and having Scott in my life has given me this assurance.

But more than just being someone who understands, he has very similar interests and dreams to my own. Scott and I have spent hours upon hours discussing how we are going to take over the world.

We discuss what products we could bring to market and different ways of making money, essentially trying to figure out how we can live our lives upside down because of our limitations. In fact, this book would not exist without Scott's help and our little brainstorming sessions, which usually happens over good food or gourmet coffee.

C.S. Lewis states: "The next best thing to being wise oneself is to live in a circle of those who are." This is what I have created for my own life: a circle of very successful and loyal individuals who can help me steer my own life and encourage me when I do not have the ability to guide myself.

THE FELLOWSHIP OF THE RAGING SLOTH

When I was in college, a group of guys and I founded the rugby team at Baylor University. None of us had any clue what we were doing, but it was a real challenge and extremely enjoyable. Even after a broken nose and several stitches, I have always enjoyed watching rugby matches and follow world cup matches and international play as much as possible when they are televised.

It was through my love of the game that I was introduced to the All Blacks, the New Zealand national rugby team. They are the winningest national rugby team of all time, and their record is so impressive they have the best winning percentage of any sports team EVER.

There is no other sports team that is more prolific and dominating than the All Blacks. The LA Lakers, the New England Patriots, the NY Yankees, and Manchester United cannot compare in their respective sports to what the All Blacks have accomplished in rugby through the years.

One of the more fascinating aspects of the All Blacks is their pregame ritual. Being from New Zealand, before every game they march out to the middle of the field and perform the Haka, a traditional dance of the native Maori tribes. A version of this dance can be traced back to the team's earliest matches in the early 1900's. If you search this dance on YouTube and watch this ritual performed by the team, it is mesmerizing, frightening, and powerful.

Not to take anything away from the phenomenal athletes that play for the New Zealand national team, but I wonder how much performing such an intense pregame ritual plays into their success. It must be phenomenal to come together as one unit before the game even begins and get the entire team on the same page in such a powerful manner.

All Blacks halfback T.J. Perenara explained the impact of the Haka: "Since I was growing up, the Haka was about the people I was with. It was about us being together. It wasn't too much about the crowd or the opposition. It was more for the camaraderie of each other. A lot of people envision it as a war dance. The way I see it, it's something to unify us as a team."

I believe the chant speaks volumes about how they perform during the match. It is the ultimate example of uniting your fellowship in a powerful experience to move forward for a common goal. It demonstrates the "irrational commitment" to one another.

The point is that this book wouldn't exist, and I wouldn't be here, or really understand how to live my life at all, let alone upside-down, if it weren't for the people in my life. This was never, and will never be, a solitary effort.

Any *success* I've achieved has only come through their support of me and my goals. It has also come through me being able to share in their successes.

The fellowship keeps me focused, helps me keep the train on the tracks, and helps me stay on the path, even though there were many, many times I wanted to run away. It always seems easier to run away than to chase my dream. The fellowship keeps me pointed toward my dream.

THE CHALLENGE OF FELLOWSHIP

This will be your challenge: to find your fellowship, your community. It may already exist around you and you just have not realized it, or it may be something you need to be intentional in discovering. Either way, if you are going to succeed in life, if you are going to live your life upside-down, then you need to be able to share it with a group around you.

When you are creating your goals and shaping your definition of success, you need to be able to incorporate a vision for your community. How are they going to support you? What are your weaknesses where you need to lean on others for support? What do you need from them to be successful? How are you going to return the favor and support them in their successes?

This is not just all about you, but a collaborative community where you each share in one another's lives and successes and hold one another up in failures.

If you can incorporate your community into your goals and definition of success, you are creating a more sustainable foundation for success. Moreover, you will have a group of people around you to share in your accomplishments. It is a greater satisfaction to share your triumphs than to launch a business or product and not have anyone with whom you could celebrate. This is why you need to enter into a community with others in order to succeed.

I cannot overstate this enough—if you do not have a community, if you do not have the support you need, you will not succeed. You cannot live life upside-down on your own.

There will be times you may need to go out on your own, but those must be quick-trip missions to accomplish whatever it is you need to see transpire. Then you must quickly return to your fellowship and community in order to achieve the ultimate success.

Becoming a Raging Sloth could be one of the greatest transformations you make in your life. It could not only change your view of success, but it could change your attitude, your relationships, and how you view yourself, all of which require the help of others around you in order for you to succeed in this process called life.

9

STEP SIX:
ENTERING THE DANGER ZONE

Taking Intentional Risks

Highway to the danger zone. Gonna take you. Right into the danger zone. ~ Kenny Loggins, Danger Zone

A sloth usually only comes down from the trees once a week for the sole purpose of using the restroom. While this situation makes me ponder such questions as, *how do they hold it so long? And why not stay in the trees?* The more pressing question is, *why do sloths put their lives in danger to simply use the bathroom?*

While on the jungle floor, the sloth is more susceptible to predators roaming around the forest. And since a sloth is a sloth, they do not have the ability to outrun, outmaneuver, or in any way try to escape if they come upon a predator on the forest floor.

Researchers really do not have a true understanding of why the sloth leaves the comfort of the trees to climb all the way down to the jungle floor and expose themselves to preda-tors for the sole purpose of a much-needed potty break.

Some researchers believe they are simply trying to displace their scent. By burying their waste on the jungle floor, they are keeping the scent out of the trees and not exposing their home to a predator's activities. Whatever the case may be, the sloth is very committed to entering this danger zone for a very particular purpose.

As a Raging Sloth, if we too are going to be successful, then we need to enter those "danger" areas of our lives to take care of necessary business, even if we're not comfortable. These would be those areas of your life you have avoided for many years.

Your danger zone may be public speaking, asking others for help, selling a product, putting yourself out there for criti-cism, or having the tough conversations with your spouse, child, or parent. Whatever your danger zone is, avoiding it limits your overall success in life. What immediately come to mind when you think about the danger zones in your life?

Part of being successful is embracing these areas as a com-ponent of the process, knowing they are danger zones but taking the risk anyway.

The risk you take in entering the danger zone is great, but it's far worse to never attempt to enter at all. Your growth, experience, and success will never happen outside the dan-ger zone.

TRUE HEROES

Through the Knights of Heroes camp, I have met some unbelievably awesome kids and moms who gave the ultimate sacrifice of losing a father and husband. I have also had the honor to work beside amazing men and women at the camp who serve in our armed forces.

I've had the opportunity to be exposed to stories from our campers of the bravery, sacrifice, and honor of men who fought with their lives to keep our country free. These are stories I never heard from the media, and frankly, had no idea existed.

Before this camp, I had no comprehension of what our men and women were facing in battle, how they were putting their lives on the line, and the strength and courage each of them possessed. What I have learned from these stories—both, of those we have lost and of those still living—is of unbelievable strength during a time of loss. They have also taught me how to face my own fears.

These men and women have served our country in Iraq and Afghanistan heading into some of the most brutal and dangerous territories we currently face. But they went in with conviction, strength, purpose, and drive.

When wives or children relay to me their stories or I read their stories retold in books, I realized that these men and women rarely questioned their mission. I began to realize, when they were deployed they would let their instincts take over because they had endured months of training for this very task.

This is the trait that fascinated me most. These men and women were never openly afraid to enter the danger zone, even though fear was present, because they had been properly trained to enter the danger zone effectively and efficiently.

Their years of training and reinforcement for this precise scenario allowed them to enter these dangerous areas with confidence and skill. Whether it was from the training they received before they were deployed or the constant repetition they faced on a daily basis in completing their assigned duties while deployed, they had become masters in their relevant fields.

What this made me realize is I can more easily and readily face my own fears if I train myself to enter my own danger zones. I can better confront the challenge in front of me if I'm properly prepared to face the challenge.

AVOIDING YOUR DANGER ZONE

The lack of training and knowledge was one of the main reasons I avoided my own danger zones. One area that suffered because of this mentality was my physical well-being. After my hip replacement, I resigned myself to a somewhat sedentary lifestyle. I was overly afraid I would damage or hurt my hip and its surrounding area. I was deathly afraid of adding any more pain to my life. I would only exercise up to a point. At the smallest observance of pain or discomfort, I would immediately stop.

I lived this way until a physical therapist explained I was making matters worse by not pushing through some of the pain. By stopping at the smallest hint of pain or discomfort, my muscles were not firing correctly, my bones were getting out of alignment, and my joints were not getting the full range of movement they needed.

I soon began the process of pushing through this dreaded danger zone. Let me tell you, it sucked! The pain was brutal, I was exhausted, and I kept asking myself what I was doing.

After about two weeks of utter fatigue and pain, I eventually called my old college roommate, Matt, who is a physical therapist and a part of my fellowship. He reassured me I was fine and I would not do any damage to the hip. His calm reassurance was very key in my continuing on with this process. Otherwise, I probably would have quit because it was affecting my entire life.

Based on Matt's advice, I kept going, and soon I began to see results. Once I started pushing through the pain, I became stronger, more limber, and I gained more balance. If you knew me, you'd know those last two traits have never been a strong point.

I had been avoiding going into this danger zone because of a legitimate fear of pain. But by avoiding pushing through the pain, I was putting my body in a worse condition and setting myself up for more pain and discomfort. This is the funny thing about danger zones: by avoiding them, you can unintentionally make your life more miserable.

EXCUSES IN OUR DANGER ZONE

One of the biggest mistakes I have made personally and professionally is the "I'll do it my way" syndrome. I watch videos of successful people, see how they did things, read their content, and then think, "I'll do it my way." I like what they say, but I'm not like them and I got this.

While it's true I'm not like the people I watch in the videos (which is why I defined success for myself), it does not mean their methods are not sound. If many people have completed a proven process to get the results I am looking for, then I cannot disregard what they are saying simply because part of what they discuss enters into one of my danger zones.

For me, this is sales. In the context of the business world, with a proven product, I was very well versed and would often be invited by a client to come pitch. I actually loved it and was pretty good at the delivery.

But cold-calling or asking people I know for something is a process I hate with every fiber of my being. I will literally break out in hives, start sweating, and fumble my words if I have to ask someone for something, or worse yet, ask a stranger.

You would think this would be easy with our Knights of Heroes camp when I go stumping for the organization. This is an awesome camp for a great cause, and everyone I talk to loves it and wants to see how to get involved.

But there have been times I have gone up to celebrities or individuals you would know from TV, sports, or movies to see if they could assist us. The way I acted would make you think I was robbing them or asking for their firstborn child. I even walk away thinking, "I'm an idiot," even though their response is, "That sounds great. Here is my contact information. I look forward to hearing from you."

I have successfully avoided this specific danger zone of my life so long I can easily justify reasons for not entering this area. I turn my personal doubts into excuses for not engaging in this activity. But in the process of not entering, I am denying myself full and complete success because I am only halfway attempting to complete my goals.

No matter what type of book I write or product I try to create, in our modern society, it will not simply sell itself. Our society no longer exists in this automated sales and marketing structure of years past. In order to sell anything, I have to cut through the clutter to make my product stand out. I have to train myself to be confident enough in order to enter this area effectively so I can be successful.

FACING YOUR DANGER ZONE

I recently had the opportunity to see my daughter Presley walk through one of her danger zones. Presley is thirteen years old and an extremely beautiful, loving, and vivacious young lady. But she is dreadfully afraid of speaking in public.

In fact, she does not even do well around strangers. She will be her loud, boisterous self when we are talking alone, but if a stranger appears, you can physically see her close off. Presley has an innate shyness, and it takes her a while to warm up to those she does not know.

This past Christmas, our pastor asked our family to read some scripture for the Christmas Eve service. Knowing Presley's abhorrence for public speaking, and my inability to pass up a good joke, I told her the pastor called and wanted her to read a passage, alone, at the Christmas Eve service.

As soon as those words left my mouth, Presley's breathing became more rapid, and her entire demeanor from head to toe slumped. I believe a rash started breaking out on her face, and she looked like she had seen a ghost.

But to her credit, through gasping breaths, she said she would do it. At this point, I reassured her the entire family would be up there with her so she would not be alone in front of the audience speaking. I am not sure this was reassuring to her, but at least someone would be by her side to catch her if she passed out.

On Christmas Eve, Presley had her piece of paper in hand with the passage typed out, and was prepared to read. When the time came, she stepped up to the microphone with the rest of the family, and she read her scripture as eloquently as possible. This was in front of over 600 people who attended the service.

I was proud of Presley's attempt to read in front of this crowd. But I was extremely proud of her for not letting her fear be an excuse in attempting something difficult. What I reassured Presley about public speaking is "you don't have to like public speaking, but you still have to be able to do it at certain times."

This was comforting to her, as this was a task that she avoided at all costs. But when the time came, she still needed to enter this danger zone effectively. You may never enjoy entering your own danger zone, but you cannot always live life avoiding it.

What I needed to do was take my own advice if I was going to launch a successful business. I was going to have to enter the danger zone, be aware of predators, and do the work necessary in order to make headway.

I had to resist the mentality of saying, "That is great, but it is not me." This is a poor excuse and will get you nowhere. I had studied and learned enough at this point that I knew there were certain cold-calling aspects of the process I was not going to be able to avoid. But I did not jump right in, for I was afraid I would break out in one gigantic rash over my entire body.

I started small, with a few e-mails here and there, reaching out slowly, trying to get comfortable. At this point, what I was getting in return from the individuals was less important than getting comfortable and making small wins. Much like the sloth hitting the ground and then taking the time to look around until it knows it is safe, once I was able to essentially get my feet stable, I began to reach out more and more. I cast my net farther and farther to get a greater reach with my business. It wasn't easy. I did not like it, and I still don't like it, but I know it is a necessary part of the process.

TAKING RISKS

When entering your danger zone, you have to be able to take risks. No one has ever succeeded without taking some type of risk in their life. This is the whole point of the sloth going to the jungle floor. It is an inherent risk. If you always play it safe in everything you attempt, then you will not sail very far. Without risk, you'll have a life, but you won't be living an adventure.

Living the upside-down life of a Raging Sloth is inherently risky. It will not come easily because you always think living right-side up is safe. You are going to have to take risks, but take them knowing you will fail in certain areas.

Part of your plan is to build in these failures in order to take a step back, pick yourself up, and go at it again. Do not run from failures but embrace them like your limitation. You are strong, and you have endured more than the average individual. Do not let the fear of failure cause you to never risk.

If you are content to simply let life happen to you, take the easy way out, and always fall back to what is comfortable, then do not complain about the results. Whether it is with your family, your business, your career, or a side project, you are going to have to take some risks in order to meet your goals and see success on your terms. It may be risky simply getting off the couch in order to accomplish the necessary activities for success, but you must calculate the outcomes against the risks.

Once I realized that I needed to stop playing it safe with my hip, I began to take risks physically. They were calculated risks, and I still played it safe as much as possible, but I did risk. I started mountain biking again; I snowboarded for the first time in five years; and in the process, I felt like I was coming back alive. There is joy in those risks, and it is worth taking them when they force you to look at life differently. To live life more freely.

HOW TO ENTER THE DANGER ZONE

You have just gone through the last few chapters in finding out your limitations and your passions and understanding your definition of success. With this specific knowledge, you also need to understand your danger zone.

What is it about life, business, or success that you fear the most? Selling, putting yourself out there, being vulnerable, failing, or not trying? Is it raising children, being a better spouse, or living a better life in general?

You need to identify your danger zones and do research to figure out how you can prepare yourself to enter them effectively and efficiently. By knowing your own specific danger zone, what you are doing is finding the tools to help you succeed. You are educating yourself, building yourself up, and creating a buffer to make your time in the danger zone limited, but more successful.

STEP 1: PREPARE

The first step in entering your danger zone is to prepare. Take the time to identify your danger zones, understand how they affect you, and acknowledge the ways you make up excuses to avoid them. This is an area where you need to be brutally honest with yourself about your fears.

STEP 2: BE HONEST

You also need to make sure you are being honest with how your limitations may be affecting your perception of your danger zones. If you do not acknowledge your danger zones appropriately, then you will continue to avoid them and thus sabotage your success.

I could make up numerous believable excuses as to why I should not reach out to other people. I could always use my pain as a reason to not move forward. But my avoidance of this area and my inability to prepare properly has caused several projects to fail miserably. I had to be honest with myself about what I was avoiding and why. That way, I could address the problem properly and prepare myself to enter the situation confidently.

STEP 3: EDUCATE YOURSELF

Next, you need to educate yourself. For me, it was a matter of finding tried-and-true, successful, specific processes to help me reach out to people and grow my business. For you, it may be public speaking. If so, attend a public speaking course like the SCORRE Conference. If it is fear of technology or social media, find some courses to help you understand what you are doing or how to do it better.

Do not be afraid to admit you can't do something. Technology can be challenging for many people. Hire someone to help you understand it better, but don't just turn everything over to them. Work with them so you know and understand what is happening in case they move on to other projects.

You are investing in your weaknesses in order to be successful. You do not have to become a computer programmer, but gain enough knowledge to be comfortable in having conversations in this specific arena.

STEP 4: FACE YOUR FEAR

The next step you need to address is to face your fear. When you went through the preparation step, you asked the question of understanding how this specific danger zone affects you. Now you need to flush this out.

How will you face your fear? Does your fear make you not want to call someone, make you a recluse, or make you break out in hives? If so, when you enter your danger zone, how will you address these side effects? Knowing how they affect you can help you get around these obstacles long before you enter your danger zone.

STEP 5: ENGAGE YOUR FELLOWSHIP

Now you need to put your fellowship on alert. There is no greater time to engage your fellowship than when you are entering your danger zone. Give your fellowship the details. They can be there for guidance, for prayer, to bounce ideas off of, to grab you by the shoulders when you want to run, or to be stern when you say you don't want to do it.

If you have set up your fellowship appropriately, then you have the ability to use them during this crucial time. If you have the right backup, it can make all the difference in the world so that when you enter the danger zone, you have the confidence to be successful.

If it had not been for Matt, I would have quit my physical therapy because it was too painful and difficult. His simple advice to keep at it allowed me to push through the uncomfortable part of my therapy to see results.

STEP 6: ENTER YOUR DANGER ZONE

You now need to enter your danger zone. You have avoided it long enough. Now you have taken the time to adequately prepare and train yourself to be successful. Take the first step and make the right decisions in order to be successful. You need to make sure you are prepared enough to enter the danger zone, but do not make excuses for not entering this crucial area of your life.

The last step is to have a backup plan. What happens when you enter the danger zone and it does not go as planned (which is highly likely)? What are you going to do? Running is not an option. If you create an appropriate backup plan first, then you will be less likely to run when the situation goes south.

What you want to think about in this arena is how you will respond if things don't go as planned. Can you look at this as a learning experience? Is there an appropriate follow-up method to your process, or do you need to go back at it again but change your strategy?

Have a backup plan every time you enter your danger zone and you will add to your preparation to ensure success. Otherwise, you are going to take a hit-and-run—meaning, you probably won't enter this danger zone again after the first unsuccessful try, which is not the correct solution.

By entering the danger zone, you will always learn something about yourself. If nothing else, you will overcome one of your greatest fears and possibly get a much greater understanding of yourself and your path to success.

If you can simply look at the danger zone in your life as another challenge instead of an overarching obstacle, you might find out you are better at it than you imagined.

If you don't come down from the trees every once in a while, your success will be limited. You have to be willing to go over the edge to understand the entirety of what you can accomplish. You may have limitations, but this does not mean you run from the hard stuff. It is even more important that you plant a strong foot down and do what needs to be done using proven methods in order to accomplish your goals.

10

STEP SEVEN: SHIFTING WEIGHT

Learning to Be Flexible and Giving Yourself Grace

Failed plans should not be interpreted as a failed vision. Visions don't change, they are only refined. Plans rarely stay the same, and are scrapped or adjusted as needed. Be stubborn about the vision, but flexible with your plan. ~ John C. Maxwell

Let me start by saying I am not flexible. Secondly, this is an understatement. Some funky genetic marker that has been passed down from generation to generation through the Eaton family limits our flexibility by birth. The second rule of our house, after the first which is "run if you see daddy run," is that if you see daddy doing splits, you need to call 911 immediately. No questions asked—just call the ambulance.

Unlike me, the sloth has the uncanny ability to contort itself into many different poses in order to fulfill different needs. It could be the lack of muscles they have in their bodies that allows this to happen, but regardless, it allows them to flex into sleeping, eating, and mating positions as the situation requires.

If you are going to be a successful Raging Sloth, then you need to be flexible. And within this flexibility be able to give yourself some grace. Part of being a Raging Sloth is not conforming to the mold of other animals. In other words, we do not want to function like everyone else.

IMPORTANCE OF FLEXIBILITY

In Jeff Goins's book *The Art of Work*, there is a chapter where he discusses pivot points. For example, in basketball, after you pick the ball up from a dribble, you cannot keep moving, but you can pivot on one foot.

"Although you are confined to where you are and how many steps you can take, at no point are you locked into any direction. That's the beauty of the move. Even when all other opportunities are exhausted, you can always pivot." Jeff's idea of pivoting is absolutely crucial in being flexible with your limitation.

When you do not have control over your circumstances, you have to be flexible and give yourself grace. I do not get the luxury of being able to put the more challenging pain days on the calendar in order to work around them.

I have to be flexible enough to work around what is given to me on any given day. I work around the pain and give myself grace if this is the reason I did not complete my goals for the week. If you beat yourself up for not functioning like everyone else, you do nothing to add to your success or to live an enjoyable life.

Like most people with a limitation, you tend to put a heavy burden on yourself. In trying to "fit in" or have people not notice your limitation, you work hard, you press forward, and you try to do what it takes in order to get it right.

But when it does not go right, you place a lot of guilt on yourself for the failure. You carry the unnecessary burden of failure on your shoulders because you never give yourself any room to fail.

You can also create this self-fulfilling prophecy by having constant thoughts that you were bound to fail anyway because of your limitations. The common reaction to this failure is to crawl into your own little private hole to sulk.

Even if you were a 100% functioning individual, you would never get 100% of your attempts correct. Failure is a part of life. It is where you grow, understand, make adjustments, and perfect your craft. If you cannot place this in the forefront of your mind before you begin, you will be paralyzed by your failures.

Because of your limitations, you can be harder on yourself, give up more quickly, or place the blame in more extreme ways if something does not work right or turn out the way you planned. If you do not have the ability to allow yourself grace in those moments and be flexible enough to make the necessary adjustments, you will live in constant frustration.

Your failures could be the best hurdles placed in front of you, but you have to be able to look at them from a realistic standpoint, see them for what they are, and not beat yourself up over the situation.

COST OF BEING INFLEXIBLE

I can be a very driven individual if the situation is right. I will pour my entire heart and soul into a project if I believe enough in what is being produced. But I always go through a predictable pattern.

When I was feeling good, I would engage in a project, pour myself into the details, and try to make it as successful as possible—whether it was a new event, new course material, or vision casting.

But sooner or later the pain would increase, draining my energy, and I would get too tired to finish the project. I would be sidelined or derailed by the pain and become extremely frustrated in my inability to complete the project. I would then start the process all over again when I felt better.

The issue was I could not give myself any grace to be flexible. I think that deep down, I never wanted to use the pain as an excuse. I wanted to prove I was still just as capable as everyone else, instead of trying to live within my habitat. I was also living my life by another definition of success which was not my own.

I did not think others would give me the grace to fail because of my limitation. Having this type of attitude only exacerbated the situation and destroyed my self-confidence.

The inability to be flexible caused me to hit a wall at a point when I was entering a very fruitful time of my ministry. I physically felt better than I had in years. I spent the summer hashing out a vision and direction for the church, and I felt very assured of where we were heading in the fall. I was more confident and productive than any other time in my adult life.

Physically, I felt strong, and I spent my 40th birthday skydiving, rock climbing, and celebrating with friends. I was ready to take on the world. But two weeks after turning 40, my hip finally gave out.

As I mentioned before, I had my hip replaced, but my recovery was not coming along as had been explained or expected. I was not functioning at the level I had anticipated, nor had I ever been taught how to live differently. I did not know it was all right to live upside down.

During this process, most of my plans had fallen by the wayside and I had no clue what to do. I didn't know how to be flexible in my plans or give myself grace to take the time to figure out my life.

I could never reconcile how to be in pain and run a church. I only crawled deeper and deeper into my hole because I felt like my worth was dwindling. My confidence deteriorated so much, I eventually left the church and moved to another state.

Because I was inflexible, I made a very poor decision. It was not the path I should have taken, nor was it healthy for me spiritually, emotionally, or mentally. It took me years to recover from this mistake, not being able to progress forward in a healthy manner.

A decision made because I was trying to live a life by someone else's definition, and because of my inability to give myself enough grace to push through a difficult time and truly understand I did not have to live my life like everyone else.

STAY IN THE GAME

We have to be able to give ourselves enough grace to stay in the game. While we may live life upside down, this does not mean we have to isolate ourselves from others. We are simply living upside down in a habitat alongside other people who live right-side up.

When you create your plan, you are setting your goals just like everyone else. You want to succeed. You want to get better and grow. But within your goals, you are giving yourself grace to flex when necessary in order to make other plans. Your goals and definition of success are not a rigid fence built for restriction. You need to look at them more as pieces on a chessboard.

Each piece on the board is a goal you have in mind. When you are able, you move your major pieces across the board to the other side. But if your limitation blindsides you or rears its ugly head at those inconvenient times, you give yourself the grace to sit in that spot until you are able to move it forward again productively.

During this time, you may have the ability to focus on minor pieces on the board and move them accordingly because they may not be as paramount or require the energy needed for your main pieces. But you can still work on them while you are attempting to normalize your situation.

If you are able to move past your issues, you go back to your major pieces and keep moving forward. This is why I think it's necessary to have outgoing goals and incoming goals. What I have realized is that my major pieces include my outgoing goals, such as the writing, the blogs, the courses, the content, the speaking—the goals that are coming out of me, that I am creating—and they require my energy and focus. These are the areas that suffer the most when the pain increases because I lose my creativity, clarity, and objectivity.

The incoming goals are more about my self-growth, and these are the minor pieces. These include watching webinars, attending conferences, taking online courses, reading books, listening to podcasts, and any other activity wherein I am absorbing the information and material. For the most part, I can usually still engage in these tasks despite being in pain.

Not knowing how I will feel when I wake up each morning, or how I will feel as the day progresses, I always have both goals ready to move. If it is a good day, I work on the outgoing goals; I move my major pieces.

If it is a bad day, I work on the incoming goals, my minor pieces. Most days I generally wake up feeling well, so I tend to focus my time in the mornings on my outgoing goals, trying to create as much as possible.

When the afternoons come and I am not feeling as well or as creative, I spend my time watching video courses or webinars, or having coffee with friends. Those activities are still useful and beneficial to me, my work, and my life, but do not require the intensive thought energy.

HOW TO BE FLEXIBLE

When you begin to create your life plan and define your goals, you need to create these goals within the context of being flexible. No matter your situation, you always want to be able to pivot. You want to create a space where you can function appropriately and effectively, without being rigid and causing frustration.

The first way you can accomplish this task is to identify those intersections of your life where you might be hard on yourself—so you can make sure you know beforehand how to deal with them when they arise. Where are you the hardest on yourself when it comes to tasks or goals? You need to highlight this area of your life so you can act appropriately when you have to pivot.

I don't do well with outside pressures, especially when I'm in pain. If I have multiple outside resources pressuring me for a deadline or project, under normal circumstances I can respond appropriately.

But when I'm in pain, I get easily frustrated; I lose my patience, and I'm quickly agitated. When I get to this place, I usually become frustrated at myself for not being able to complete the project, or act accordingly.

In reality, I cannot forgo all outside influences in my life and simply live as a hermit—although it does sound enticing. To address this situation appropriately, I need to bring better balance to my outside projects.

I can generally handle two or three projects successfully even in pain. Beyond this number, it gets too difficult to manage and I'm no longer allowing myself enough space to be successful. I have to carefully manage my number of projects and keep them balanced against my pain levels at any given moment. It is, and always will be, a very fluid process.

Make absolutely sure you are purposefully identifying those areas of your life where you can be unusually tough on yourself, and make a plan so you can address those areas appropriately. Not allowing flexibility will always sabotage your success.

This is also true in my personal life. Under normal circumstances, I can handle changing plans, unexpected activities, or last-minute notices about events my kids have known about for months. But when the pain is overwhelming, I do not handle surprises very well. In the height of pain, the more contained my life, the easier it is for me to manage.

Knowing I don't respond well, I personally try to balance these times by trying to communicate my pain level to my family and asking my children more questions to make sure they haven't forgotten to tell me about an activity. It is not always ideal, but it reduces overall frustration and helps me pivot with my family.

To be flexible, the next step you can take is to begin making a list of outgoing and incoming goals. What are those goals that require you to produce (outgoing), and what are those areas in which you need to absorb information (incoming)?

Once you identify these goals, identify how you can balance them on any given day. Write out your goals so you can work on either type, depending on how you are feeling and how your day is progressing.

I begin each morning by writing down my "Tasks Toward Goals" on my daily planner, as outgoing goals that I need to complete each day. (The "Task Toward Goals" is found on the daily planner sheet in the Companion Guide at www.theragingsloth.com/bonus.)

These are the goals that are getting me closer to my better adventure. Then, in the Break Point area, I put down incoming goals. These are generally watching training videos, reading books, or reviewing other content. During the course of any day, if I am unable to work on one of my outgoing goals, then I adjust and move on to my incoming goals.

The next way you can be flexible is to understand the rhythms of your life. Depending on your limitation, are there parts of the day, week, or month that are better than others? When you review your life and your limitation, can you identify a pattern in your life of peaks and valleys? Is there a time of day or week in which you work better and are more productive?

When you create your life plan and fill out your daily plan, this is how you can get a jump on creating space in your life to move toward success—by knowing when you work best and what roadblocks are thrown your way, and how to be able to work around them accordingly.

Understanding this rhythm in my life is why I put my major content in the mornings. Then move to my incoming tasks in the afternoon. This allows me to accomplish my goals, and more importantly, from a personal standpoint, I still feel productive.

I have also learned that I'm not always in the greatest shape after physical therapy. This is a rhythm of my life where I do not try to plan any high-concentration activities after therapy. If I feel fine afterward, then it is just a bonus for me and I can continue on with my outgoing activities instead of moving to incoming ones.

I want to repeat this point again: these activities may seem trivial, but they are still useful and allow me to *feel productive*. This productivity goes back to my purpose, which is the greatest deterrent in fending off frustration.

Without purpose, you do not feel productive, and those are the times you begin to get down on yourself and feel useless.

I get it. I know if you live with a long-term limitation, the struggles of feeling useless can be mind-numbing at times. Being able to look around to see the baby steps you can take to feel and be more productive can be life-changing.

DOING THE PIVOT DANCE

Once you have set yourself up with a plan, clarity of your rhythms in life, and your goals, then you need to pivot when needed. You need to be flexible without the guilt. If your obstacle appears in front of you, then flex. Put down your outgoing goals and move to an incoming task.

If your obstacle becomes overbearing, then put everything down and come back to it tomorrow. This is fine. This is why you add these options to your plan on a daily basis. Do not add any more pressure to your own existence.

Like me, you probably have this mentality that if you write something down on a Monday, then you have to finish it on Monday. And just like everyone else, you always want to do your best, to eliminate all excuses—except your obstacle—to complete the tasks.

If your obstacle blocks your path, then drop what you are doing and take care of yourself or your loved ones. Putting guilt upon yourself because you have to deal with your obstacle is ridiculous and serves no purpose. This is your life, and it *is* a great life. Remember, you are living it on your terms.

The last step you need to always remember, no matter what, is to give yourself grace, because you deserve it. In fact, it is not optional. You do not get to live your life like everyone else, which is fine because you have chosen to live your life upside down.

Always remember this decision and give yourself enough grace to fail, to push the project back a day, to pick back up next week, or to start over. This is life on your terms, and part of being a Raging Sloth is to always allow grace in your life. Your life is difficult enough; there's no reason to add to the challenges by being hard on yourself.

If you allow yourself the grace and flexibility to make adjustments, you can stay on track, stay in your own habitat, and gain the rewards of success. You can reap the benefits of being useful and productive. Instead of falling into the traps of self-doubt, self-imploding, or self-sabotaging all because you have not allowed yourself the grace to see your situation clearly.

Learning to pivot will be a constant dance you need to utilize throughout your life. As a Raging Sloth, it is how you maintain an extraordinary and productive life.

11

STEP EIGHT: OWNING YOUR INNER RAGING SLOTH

Becoming the Best You

I yam what I yam. ~ **Popeye**

Sloths have a quirky facial feature that makes them look like they are always smiling. I can only guess their smile is a smirk that comes from the knowledge that they have endured and survived much longer than many other, more capable animals.

It is a unique characteristic that keeps the sloth going long after many other, much stronger and faster animals have disappeared. There is something to be said about being comfortable enough in your own skin to rise above expectations and fight against the odds.

This concept of being comfortable in one's own skin is something people with limitations can view as a curse. Because of my chronic nerve pain, my actual skin can feel like it is on fire or that electricity is shooting through the surface of my skin.

This pain, this constant struggle, makes me very uncomfortable in my own skin, and there are times when I long to be in someone else's skin, even if only for a day.

For a Raging Sloth to be successful, you have to be comfortable in your own skin, which means you need to stop comparing yourself to anyone else. You need to stop trying to be something you are not.

No one else can be an awesome Raging Sloth like you can, and you have to own this responsibility with every fiber of your being. This is success on your own terms.

STOP COMPARING

Your success can never be compared to other people. You cannot define your success by others, and more importantly, you cannot define your failures by others. Comparing yourself to others will be a constant source of frustration and you will never feel like you are enough.

You will continually tell yourself you do not have what it takes. Instead of asking yourself why you failed, you need to ask if success only comes in one color, because the answer is no—success comes in a spectrum of colors.

One of the biggest mistakes I made in my pursuit of success was constantly comparing myself to more physically capable individuals. I was consulting for Fortune 500 companies in a very fast-paced environment. I knew the material well, I could engage the client well, and I could sell the product.

But because of my physical limitations, I could not keep up the pace of my peers. I would work a full day and go back to my home or hotel completely exhausted while my peers were going out for drinks or dinner.

This became very apparent one week when I met Glenn in San Francisco for an internal business meeting. We had a meeting and dinner with the local office one night and was out late. Glenn got up early the next morning to fly to the Chicago office for the same internal meeting and dinner. Then, the next day, he flew to the New York office without ever missing a beat. All the while, I was still recovering from one late night in San Francisco.

Another leader I respect would juggle multiple projects, flying all over the East Coast, doing phenomenal work, and blazing an amazing trail, impressing everyone she met. Still another peer would go out to a casino or sightsee at night after work until the late hours, then show back up in the morning bright and ready to go. Almost everyone I worked with could keep going long after I had called it a day.

There is no way I could keep up with this type of work life.

Each night I would attempt one of two scenarios: I would try to go out with my peers to engage them and work to build the team, or I would go back to the hotel and collapse.

Even worse, some of my peers were going back to the hotel and getting back online to finish more work after dinner. This was completely beyond my physical and mental ability, and it left me frustrated because I could not keep up. I felt like a lifted SUV or truck with oversized tires attempting to compete in a race of Ferraris.

And so came the realization: I was created differently. Created for a specific purpose. I was built to do something very unique. But as long as I tried to compete with the other sports cars, I was going to be frustrated and feel inadequate, like I was not living up to others' expectations. I was also putting unnecessary expectations on myself in trying to live up to standards others were accomplishing.

However, I knew if we went off-road, none of them could keep up. I knew I had the skills and abilities to blaze a trail, do business differently and on my terms, because this was how I was made.

This is part of the Raging Sloth lifestyle; you too were built for something specific. Part of your challenge is to discover your specific function, your unique purpose. I can blaze a great big trail off-road and do things none of my other peers are capable of doing, but it is on my own trail, and I need to blaze this trail as boldly as possible.

You have to realize that when you get to the point where you stop comparing yourself to others, you are freeing yourself up to the resistance you might be facing in blazing your own trail—a trail that is based on your own abilities, gifts, and desires. By eliminating comparisons to others, you are free to be you instead of what you think you should be based on others' abilities or definitions.

IDENTIFYING COMPARISON IN YOUR LIFE

If you are going to blaze your own trail appropriately and stop the comparison, then there are four ways to know if you are comparing yourself to others. The first and most obvious sign is frustration.

Frustration is a glaring sign of comparison. You get frustrated easily because your tasks, projects, and goals are not turning out as anticipated. But beyond the lack of success, you are frustrated your life or success does not have the look or feel of what you see in others, even though you may be in the same position or place in life.

The defining difference between you and others is that you were meant to live upside down. This means either you're not working or living in the right habitat or you don't have the right attitude to succeed the way others do. It may mean you simply do not have the same drive as others, which isn't bad because your drive may be somewhere else or to do something else, but it can also contribute to your frustration.

The second sign you are comparing yourself to others is when you're unable to be happy for others successes. When a friend or colleague succeeds, especially in your field, you are jealous and can only congratulate them through gritted teeth. You may also become jealous in your personal life when a friend has a nice, shiny new object that you desire.

If you are constantly comparing your life and success to others, you are aiming for a target you will never hit. Your goal is not to reach their potential; otherwise, being genuinely happy for other people's success will be a challenge for you.

Your struggle mainly comes from the internal dialogue that states, "Why not me?" You think you have the skills and abilities for the same success, but somehow, someone else achieved the status or place you longed for.

The next time someone in your life reaches a milestone or has some success come their way, and you become jealous, ask yourself why. Do you think their success belongs to you?

Discover why you are comparing yourself to others in this situation. You also need to realize you are a Raging Sloth, and when you begin to live your life upside down, then you will achieve your own type of success on your terms. You must look at life and success from a completely different angle.

I have viewed many peers in my field whose accomplishments made me jealous. But when I peeled back the layers and began to live my life upside down, I gained a different perspective.

What I saw was that while they attained business success, their marriages were falling apart, their children stopped speaking to them, their integrity was lacking, or others spoke poorly of them behind their backs. This is not my definition of success, nor is it the life I wanted to live.

What we see on the outside of others is rarely an accurate reflection of what is happening inside. When you live upside down, your perspective changes and you can begin to see the truth behind the circumstances.

The third sign of comparison is a lack of clarity. If you are constantly comparing yourself to and trying to outdo others, then you are going to be swayed by anything that comes your way. You will let yourself be blown wherever the wind blows. The next conference, book, or process will always seem intriguing because you lack the clarity of what specific direction you should be taking. You will struggle with saying no.

The lack of clarity in your life generally means you have no plan. Being able to create a vision and plan for your life will shape clarity, which then allows you to shed your comparisons because you'll be focused on what you can do and how you will accomplish your goals.

The lack of clarity will always create a fuzzy haze on any situation you view, and you will lack the ability to see truth in the circumstance. Being crystal clear with your path eliminates the fog and illuminates your path.

The fourth sign of comparison are feelings of inadequacy. This is an issue most of us who live with a limitation or pain suffer with in general. When you are constantly comparing yourself to others with different skill sets, different energy, and fewer obstacles, you will always feel inadequate. You will never measure up to them, by their standards.

This is why you have to create a life plan on your terms. This is why you must live upside down. You are only inadequate in the unrealistic life you have created.

You cannot expect a fish to ride a bicycle. It's an unrealistic expectation. The fish makes a great fish, until you take it out of the water. You are God's masterpiece and were created for his perfect plan. You only believe you are inadequate because you are too far out of your habitat, attempting to live life as someone you are not.

Recognize where you are comparing yourself and stop the process. Begin to remove any obstacles that may be impeding your pathway to success—specifically, those obstacles that reside in your head.

BLAZE YOUR OWN TRAIL

If you recognize that you are comparing yourself unfairly to others, how do you stop the process in order to live life on your terms? You can begin the process by believing in yourself, your talents, and your abilities regardless of your circumstances. This belief in yourself will be a powerful tool in your transformation to a Raging Sloth because it will give you the power and energy to live life on your terms.

Belief in yourself allows you to find your own path. By blazing your own trail, you are no longer tied to what other people are doing, nor are you comparing yourself to their successes and lives. Blazing your own path will give you a tremendous amount of freedom because you're not being shackled to others' ideas of success.

Being able to believe in your own gifts and talents will also give you the ability to live life on your terms. You have an amazing story, and you have a gift that needs to be shared. But you have to stop hiding behind your limitation. It is time to share your gift with the world.

If you do not believe you can live differently, you will live insufficiently. You will constantly be trying to live right-side up. Your mind will tell you this is right because it is the easy path, this life is comfortable.

But your heart will vehemently disagree. You have to fight the urge to go back to what you think is comfortable. Believe in what you can accomplish by living differently in order to avoid the right-side-up life.

You also have to believe in your talents. I firmly believe God has given all of you unique, special, and life-changing talents. They will not always be obvious or noticeable, nor will you be able to discover their purposes easily, but they do exist. It is up to you to take the time and energy to discover your talents, see where they can be used, hone your skills, and apply them. These abilities are inside you, but you need to take the time and do the work to discover their purpose. Then, believe enough in yourself to use them to change the world.

DO WHAT YOU DO WELL

One area of my life where I encountered difficulty transitioning to an upside-down life was being a parent. Growing up, and early on in my marriage, I had ideas about the type of father I wanted my children to experience.

I had visions of throwing the football around or playing games of basketball with my boys and being able to run, play soccer, or sit on the floor playing house with my daughter. But those dreams were crushed before children were even in the picture.

This frustration grew when I saw other parents doing certain activities with their children, things that I couldn't do. Or when my own kids talked about someone's dad doing something awesome.

My inability to offer similar experiences to my children was an indescribable pain in my heart. Although, to my kids' credit, they have never held my pain or struggles over my head or against me, even though it has been a challenge for them.

My frustration was extremely counterproductive and becoming detrimental to my relationship with my children. I would also linger too long in negative thoughts. In order to climb out of this mindset, I had to shift my thinking to what I could do and stop hanging onto outdated dreams.

In the process of being the best father I can be, our family has turned out to be somewhat unconventional. On good days, I can participate in activities like rock climbing, mountain biking, skiing, and hiking. But most days are spent watching a movie or playing cards. Either way, I am accomplishing the most important thing I can do as a parent. I am spending time with my children and creating great memories.

I could not always be involved in these activities to the level I would have preferred, but I have always tried to simply be involved. When my daughter, Presley, began showing interest in soccer, I was not too enthused—not because I didn't like the sport since I played soccer growing up, but with nerve damage in my right foot, kicking a ball was certainly not on the top of my "yeah, let's do this" list.

When she gravitated to goalie, I had to shift my thinking again. I could not kick a ball well, but we'd go out and practice and I would throw the ball at her. It was not what I pictured in my head, but it was working. It was serving a purpose, and I was involved with my daughter—and Presley loves when I give her my undivided attention.

On the simplest level, I take one of our children out for breakfast each week before school. This is easy, low-key, and aside from sitting in some uncomfortable restaurant chairs, pretty pain-free. My kids have my sole attention and we are building memories.

My children are amazing in their understanding of my limitation and the grace they give me in more trying times. They never bring it up and never let it be an excuse. They also understand when I tell them I cannot do an activity. They may not always like it, but they understand.

What I don't want to pass on to them is the image of a father who was always on the sidelines, never involved, or lived a frustrated life because he could not live another dream.

I want to pass on to my children the image of a father who lived life to its fullest regardless of the pain, struggles, or circumstances. A father who may not have been involved in traditional ways but did not let this stop him, and who used what he did have to change their lives.

If I am able to accomplish this goal in my own life and in the lives of my children, then I have certainly achieved one of my greatest steps toward success. Within this goal, there is nothing I have to compare it to. It is my own, and it is awesome.

I may not have been able to live the life I dreamed or wanted, but all this has done is made me think harder, dream differently, and live more passionately. Life is still awesome, and that is because it is my life, on my terms. I am no longer trying to be anything other than myself. I no longer try to compare my life or success to others. I am just me, and I think I am a pretty awesome Raging Sloth.

12

STEP NINE:
ELIMINATING EXCUSES

Never Having to Say "I'm Sorry"

As a man thinketh in his heart, so is he. ~ Proverb

Let's be clear from the beginning: your limitation is not an excuse for your lack of success. I understand; I have used my pain on numerous occasions to justify my failures. But we all have excuses, and we all use them when it is convenient for us. Do any of the following excuses resonate with you?

- Ten more minutes of sleep and I will get up.

- Just one more episode on Netflix and then I will turn it off!

- It is only one donut.

- It's not you, it's me.

- I need a little me time.

- I can go to the gym tomorrow.

- As soon as life slows down, I will write that book.

- We will have kids when we are ready.

I could go on and on. Many of you can relate to what was listed and probably have an ongoing list in your head of additional excuses. The bottom line is, we all have excuses for one reason or another. But when living with an obstacle, excuses can become a debilitating crutch.

NO EXCUSES

I hate excuses!

But I feel like I've had to dole out thousands of them because of my pain. I had to explain to a new client every time I showed up why I moved slowly, why I couldn't sit still for very long, or even why I was grumpy that day. I had to tell people why I missed an event or gathering when I had a painful episode that was too overwhelming for me to be social, or why I will never help someone move even though I look very capable.

Every time I have to use one of these excuses, it eats me up inside. I don't know if it's because of my upbringing or hearing my old high school football coaches in my head yelling about what they think about excuses, which would be unrepeatable in this book.

Many people understand, but I've also had people I would consider good friends walk away and never talk to me again because I couldn't help out with some activity or do what they wanted. Either way, it always tears me up when I have to give an excuse for my behavior or absence.

This process is also challenging because I never know how I will feel on any given day. I don't know why I can ride a bike for ten miles one day, but I had to lay on the couch the day before in overwhelming pain. I don't enjoy attempting to explain this inconsistency in my life to others. I can see the suspicion in their eyes. I don't get it, but it is a reality in my daily life.

I also feel like I am having to justify my existence. Having to constantly explain my life to others is tiring, especially when I know they have no idea what I am attempting to convey to them. Telling your work why you cannot come in today. Telling your health insurance why you need another surgery or need to be on disability. Telling your friends why you cannot show up again. Constantly attempting to justify my own existence is exhausting and extremely frustrating.

What I have realized is that one of the main reasons I had to give excuses is because I was putting myself in situations that required them. I was not functioning at my full potential because I was living someone else's life, and doing so required excuses to explain why I could not keep up the pace. I had created an environment where excusing my actions was the only way I could survive and get through the day. When you are running a race you were never created to run, excuses become a survival mechanism to create the façade of a normal life.

We all too often use our limitations as a reason to excuse ourselves from an activity, which in some cases can be valid.

But we should never use them as a reason for not discovering our own success, especially if we have carefully defined our limitations and defined success on our terms. By accomplishing these two goals, we are setting ourselves up to succeed without excuses.

When you come up with an excuse, even as a thought in your head, you are limiting yourself before you even get out of the gate. Excuses can be an easy way to give up, especially when living with a limitation. Most people are going to be sympathetic to your pain and plight and understand when you cannot go any further. They will inadvertently enable you to rely on your excuses instead of accomplishing your goals.

THE DEEPER SIDE OF EXCUSES

What you generally do not comprehend about excuses is that they're usually a sign of a deeper issue or problem you are trying to mask. Amy Nordrum stated: "Frequent excuse making, however, comes with risks. A new study suggests that self-handicapping—behavior that precedes a performance and is intended to explain away any potential poor results (I didn't get around to studying math until last night)—is associated with lower motivation and achievement in students. And if professionals too often attempt to talk their way out of taking responsibility, colleagues may lose faith in them."

She went on to say, "A study by researchers at Iowa State University shows that when an employee tries to hedge against judgment for a performance by pointing to handicapping

factors (like slim resources or tight deadlines), the justifica-
tions lose credibility after just the second time."

It's important to note that you are not only losing credibility
with your peers, but you are losing credibility with yourself.
If you use your limitation as an excuse once, you will keep
using it whenever it serves your purpose. This mode of thinking will be a constant roadblock to your success.

In my inability to do my job, I was constantly coming up
with excuses that were not related to my limitation. I was
attempting to hide my limitation behind an excuse. It was
my way of not showing weakness. But was nevertheless inef-
fective and useless to my peers.

Creating an environment where you do not need excuses
is not necessarily easy. You need to be honest about your
limitation, but don't allow your limitation to be an excuse for
your lack of success. I get it, this is a difficult road. I struggled
mightily with this balance. My leg hurt, I was in legitimate
pain, which limited me from doing certain activities and kept
me from running with the big dogs.

But I was attempting to run a race I was incapable of competing in effectively. This came to a head when I went back
into the consulting world and was traveling back and forth
each week between Phoenix and Delaware.

In the beginning, my limitation was not a big deal other than
being a slight inconvenience. But a couple of months into the
project, my leg started swelling and causing a tremendous

amount of pain, especially when I sat for long periods of time on an airplane or in a conference room.

I told myself this was just temporary and once I could get a couple of weeks of rest, the inflammation would go away and I could get back into the game. In my mind, I could handle the travel. I had to prove I could do what was expected of me.

Eventually I took those couple of week's rest, and nothing changed. The pain was still there, my leg was still inflamed, and it still caused issues when I sat for long periods of time. After some extensive research by doctors, it was determined that my issue was not going to just go away. The only way I could keep traveling and working in my current job was to deal with the pain.

While I have always guarded against using my pain as an excuse, I had to come to grips with the reality I was facing—and I was facing this reality because I had placed myself in circumstances beyond my control.

I was working at a job where I had no control over where I went, what I worked on, or where my career was headed. I was constantly having to make excuses because of the environment I had placed myself in.

CONFRONTING EXCUSES

I was fully capable and functional to work, but I struggled when attempting to fulfill someone else's expectations and schedule. I had to do the work on my terms. There were days I had to sit in a recliner or stand to use the computer.

I could sit, or stand, at my computer for hours typing away and writing stories, but I had to do it on my time. This meant days where I had to start early in the morning and take long breaks in the afternoon in order to complete a given task.

I also learned when bad days hit—and they would hit hard— I would line up more activities where I was consuming information instead of trying to create information. In learning my limitations, it became quite clear that when I was in pain, I did not concentrate very well, nor did I even make sense. My mind would become clouded and I had difficulty listening and processing information.

When I take this situation and apply it to circumstances I can control, I can be productive and successful. In another environment, I can appear lazy, uncooperative, and useless because I cannot function as expected in this career field or as my peers. Thus, I feel I have to make an excuse.

When I go through the steps to define success for myself, understand and work within my limitations, and work within my own habitat, I am giving myself the ability to be successful and not make excuses.

It was also helpful to take a step back and see where I had been making excuses in my own life. When I started writing them down, I began to give life to them, and in giving life to them, I was able to deal with them appropriately.

One example of an excuse I was always making, yet never realized, is in the area of risk. Over the years of pain, I became averse to risk-taking. In the process of trying to live a safe life, I always took the path of least resistance.

Whatever was the easiest path to take or the easiest choice to make was usually where you would find me. Whether this was a choice with my career, my family, relationships, or activities, I was always choosing the easy way out. I was walking around with my life firmly encased in a thick layer of Bubble Wrap.

This excuse was the same reason I was not living in my habitat. Because I had chosen to live a life devoid of risk, I was not taking the necessary chances to allow me to succeed. I was not looking at life correctly. I wanted to put myself in a position where I did not have to make excuses, but in the process, I was simply taking myself out of life altogether.

It took quite a bit of reflection for me to realize how badly my desire to play it safe had affected my life and sidetracked my family and career. But through the process of taking the risk to move my life into the environment where I knew I would thrive and be successful, I was also eliminating the excuses that I had been relying on for years.

EXPOSING YOUR EXCUSES

If you are going to become an effective Raging Sloth, then you need to begin to expose the excuses in your life for what they are. What excuses are you using in your life to hide your ability to succeed? Do you convince yourself that:

- You will not succeed because of your limitation.

- You are not good enough.

- Your limitation will never allow you to do anything worthwhile.

Every one of these excuses sends you down the path of a false journey.

If you want to begin to bring your excuses to light, then write them down and expose them. When you write them down, you are setting them in front of you for the sole purpose of being able to deal with them appropriately. This may be a process you do on your own, or you can sit down with a spouse or close friend and have them help you identify those areas where you have used excuses to limit your success. The excuses you want to concentrate on in this exercise are those you use to hinder your success because of your limitation.

Once you have written down your excuses, the next step is to discover why they are excuses. Within this exercise, you want to be able to look at each one from every angle possible. Do you have control over the current situation that elicits the excuse? Do you have the ability to put yourself in a better situation? Are you using your excuse as a crutch to not attempt your goals? You need to examine your excuse from every angle in order to fully understand why you use it in the first place.

After you have identified why you use your excuse, you want to write a plan to eliminate the excuses. How are you going to move beyond the excuse in order to live your life upside down? The answer may be a simple change of habit in your life. It might entail rethinking how you deal with family or friends, or even your career. Or it might be a slow process over a period of time in order to place yourself in the position to not have to make excuses.

In the process of identifying your excuses, you may be incorporating the elimination of excuses into your overall life plan. When you review your life plan, how does eliminating excuses fit into the overall process? Is your life plan the result of eliminating excuses? Either way, you want to be able to have a specific, trackable plan to help you live life on your terms.

The most difficult part will be changing your habitat and behavior to no longer need excuses. Since you have identified them appropriately and have created a plan to move away from your excuses, now it is time to act on it. Put your plan in action and deal with your excuses head-on so you will not have to trip over them again in your journey to success.

The overall goal, in order to avoid sabotaging your pathway to success, is to refrain from using your limitations as an excuse for failure. You eventually want to completely remove the excuses from your vocabulary. Put yourself in a position to succeed by not giving life to those excuses anymore.

By choosing this approach, you can stay focused on your goals, be flexible with your goals, understand your limitations, and truly be successful. Otherwise, you will always sabotage your results and outcomes because you will always have an excuse ready no matter what comes your way.

OWNING THE RAGING SLOTH

You are a Raging Sloth. You are not going to settle, you are not going to let obstacles get in your way of success, and you are no longer going to make excuses for your actions. This is your life, and although your circumstances may suck, life is good and you are going to make it awesome.

It's time for you to fully own your circumstances and position in life. The obstacles you face may not be fair, may not be fun, or may be a burden, but your position in life does not matter. What matters now is what you do with what you have been given. You are no longer going to sit around and feel sorry for yourself, or wait for others to hand life to you on a silver platter.

You have a tremendous gift, an amazing ability that the world needs to see. If you don't take your rightful place in presenting your talents to the world, then we will all miss out on what you have to offer. Do not let your limitation, your place in life, or your excuses get in the way of becoming what you were created to be. You are a Raging Sloth, and now it is time to live life out loud in extraordinary abundance.

PART 3

BALANCE YOUR LIFE: LIFE IN YOUR HABITAT

Maintaining the Life of a Raging Sloth

13

THE BALANCE OF
THE RAGING SLOTH

Achieving Effective Balance In Life

Next to love, balance is the most important thing.
~ John Wooden

Paul was finally living his dream. He had a twenty-five-year career that would provide a nice retirement, and a wife and two young kids by his side watching his dreams become a reality. Paul found love late in life and was enjoying catching up on what it meant to be a family man.

Paul had always been great with kids and was a very personable and caring individual to be around. He deserved this time in his life to enjoy what he had seen from the sidelines for too long.

But Paul's life was about to be turned upside down. His wife filed for divorce and left him caring for their two young children. Paul had been working a job that required him to travel, and this was the only life he had known. But he knew he could not keep up the travel and be the father he wanted to be to his children, especially during this crucial time in their lives.

At a point in most men's careers when they begin to structure their lives for retirement, Paul walked away from his job in order to be a better father to his children. Now in his late forties, he was venturing into a new career, a new phase in life, and a new lifestyle. Paul needed to make sure he kept balance in his life if he was going to restore all the areas of his life that unexpectedly fell apart.

A SLOTH'S ATTEMPT AT BALANCE

National Geographic explorer Lucy Cooke wrote: "A sloth's body and biology are perfectly evolved to expend minimum energy. Curved claws and a strong grip allow them to hook on and hang—like a living hammock. An efficient design means they only need half the muscles of mammals their size. Their metabolism is half that expected of mammals a similar size and their body temperature is a few degrees lower than other mammals. They lack the ability to shiver and are known to bask in the sun, like cold-blooded reptiles. Resembling the actions of lizards who need to warm up in the morning to get moving."

The sloth's home life is pretty comfortable, and easy, for that matter. They spend their days in the trees with arms that are uniquely designed to hug a tree, and create their own portable hammock to be used anywhere as needed. Of all the unique gifts nature has within the animal kingdom, I cannot think of a better adaptation I would not mind utilizing.

This unique quality of being able to create its own built-in hammock helps the sloth create perfect balance for rest, which is counter to the fact that sloths do not have good balance. Researchers have found that the semicircular canals in the sloth's inner ear are almost half the size of an animal with similar proportions.

Scientists also found the size of the ear canal differs even among various sloth species. The reason, they believe, is the fact that sloths move so slowly, they have no need for balance the way more swiftly moving animals do. Nevertheless, the sloth again makes the most of the gifts it has been given in order to balance its life appropriately.

ACHIEVING YOUR PERFECT BALANCE

Part of becoming a Raging Sloth is being able to achieve balance, even when given less abilities compared to others, in order to keep all parts of life in perfect harmony. I'm not completely sure if *balance* is the right word here because achieving perfect balance is almost impossible. But anyway, now that you have figured out how to live upside down, you need to learn how to effectively maintain this lifestyle.

When you have to balance work, home, hobbies, children, spouses, finances, friends, church, community activities, children's activities, and anything else you have in your life, it resembles attempting to spin plates on a pole.

You have probably seen circus performers, or street acts, spinning plates on fifteen poles sticking up out of the ground.

For a brief while, these plate-spinners run up and down the line of poles getting the plates balanced and spinning. Once they get to the point where all the plates are spinning at one time, the plate-spinners take a ceremonious bow.

What happens when you stop spinning a plate? It falls and shatters. This is what the balancing act looks like in our own lives. No one really wants their work, marriage, finances, friendships, or children to crash. But unless you are putting enough energy into each plate, they will certainly falter and begin to topple.

This is where the balance comes in. For the most part we put our energy wherever it is most needed at the time. We automatically rush to the plate that is beginning to topple. We dump a tremendous amount of energy into the wobbling plate, furiously attempting to get it back spinning. Then we take a look around to see if another plate is about to fall.

Marriages, relationships with our children, and friendships will begin to fall and crumble when we put too much time and energy into another endeavor. This plate can be our career, especially if we are trying to get a business or new venture off the ground.

Our relationships or career can also begin to topple if our limitation is consuming too much of our energy. We are infusing all of the energy we have into one plate to the detriment of the others, and eventually they start to topple and fall to the ground shattering into pieces.

When we fall short in a certain area, it's usually because of our inability to define success properly. We are attempting to live out someone else's idea of success and our plates begin to wobble.

If we are not working in the right place, or not relating to others appropriately, our frustration will boil over to different plates. Eventually, all our plates are going to fall because we're not properly balanced.

Those of us who live with a limitation have the unfortunate yearning to overcompensate. You push too hard at work, in your relationships, or with your hobbies just to prove to everyone else that you are good enough, can get the job done, or are worth having around.

Maybe you're too hard on yourself because you are unable to get up to participate in the activities. You then restrict yourself to isolation in order to avoid becoming a burden to others. But the end result is usually exhaustion or frustration, neither of which will serve you well.

Deep inside, you may feel inadequate because of your limitation. You feel like less of a person and possibly insufficient when on the job or with your family. At times it can be a challenge just to have the motivation and energy to get out of bed.

In some cases, you try to balance too many plates in order to fill this void and prove your worth. You tell yourself everything is all right, but you really have no comprehension of what "all right" looks like. You keep adding plates in an attempt to justify your existence.

AN UNBALANCED LIFE

When you live with a limitation outside your habitat, you have to constantly justify your existence to those around you. You must explain your pain to a doctor, your insurance, your company, family, and friends. This constant justification adds confusion in your life by repeatedly bringing up the questions of "am I good enough", "am I a burden", "do I have what it takes", or "why bother." The incessant questioning of your very existence will gradually throw your life out of balance.

One of my greatest failures was my ill-fated attempt to balance life. I was trying to keep too many plates spinning in an attempt to impress or to prove that my existence mattered by a false definition of success. All of my plates began to unravel around the time of my hip replacement surgery.

I had received my hip replacement while working as a full-time pastor. The months leading up to the replacement were extremely painful. The hospital could not get me into surgery for three months, and the doctors did not want me taking pain medication before the surgery because it thinned my blood.

The pain I endured during this time was extremely overwhelming. My wife and I had to sit our children down and explain to them that daddy was not himself. I had no patience, I was agitated, and I could not think clearly. The filter most of us have in our heads which tells us to take a breath, not overreact, or simply let it roll off our backs is completely obliterated when you suffer in intense pain over long periods of time.

Having this conversation with my children was the single most difficult talk I've ever had to engage in. I am grateful they understood my circumstances, even at a young age.

But my heart was almost shattered when one day, my oldest child looked at me through tear-stained eyes and said, "I know you don't mean it; it's because of your pain." I had exploded on him for no reason. Pain unbalances your life in a very extreme manner.

I thought that once the replacement was complete, the pain would go away and I could get back to my life. After the surgery, I had to sit on the couch for a month letting my incisions heal before starting my physical therapy.

The therapy was going well at first and I was progressing. But I eventually hit a wall. I'd say I only had about 50% of the strength I had before surgery.

But I could not really define this, nor could I verbalize very well how I felt. I jumped back into my work and tried to go full steam ahead with plans, visions, and activities. I thought this would help me get my life back on track, or at least take my mind off my discomfort.

But having fought the pain for so long, I realized I had nothing left to give. I was completely depleted because I was trying to juggle too many plates instead of focusing on my family and healing.

Being successful, and becoming a Raging Sloth, means keeping all of the plates spinning at the same time without neglecting any one plate. This requires strategy and taking your time with each of your plates. You have to understand the reason behind each plate and why you have them spinning.

You can accomplish this by being strategic with your number of plates. As a person with limitations, you need to know your limits and fully utilize the wonderful power of the word "no." How many plates can you successfully spin at any given time? This, again, will vary for different people and at different stages in life.

But this is why you have goals—so your plates are aligned with what you want in life. The number of plates you have does not matter as much as being able to successfully spin all your plates with the same amount of vigor. You must be able to give each plate the attention it deserves.

A CONTINUOUS PROCESS

To successfully attain balance you will need to constantly monitor your plates. Does a plate need to be dropped or removed? Is your situation changing, and thus requiring you to reevaluate your plates and adapt to the new circumstances?

You should not be locked into any of your plates aside from a few necessary ones we will discuss later. It is important to be able to distinguish which plates can be put down for a season in order to address your needs or because of changes in your limitations.

Post-hip replacement, I could not see this path clearly. I needed to put down several plates in order to heal properly, but my focus was too clouded to even notice which plates were falling.

There are various points in your life that are fluid, and your circumstances will change. Your kids will grow and move out of the house. Your job, or your spouse's job, may take you to another state or city. You need to know when it is time to put down a plate, or possibly pick up another one. Understanding the seasons and rhythms of your life can be exceptional work in keeping the necessary balance in your life.

When living with a limitation that you have no control over, the key is to know when to pivot. You need to know when to adjust to the ever-changing ebb and flow of life. I do not get any say about when I have a bad day and when the pain is more intolerable than another day.

But what I have learned is how to adjust my schedule when I have a bad day. What can I push off until tomorrow? What can I do that can take my mind off the pain? How can I change my plates in order to be more effective?

If you can keep your plates in balance and spinning correctly, you will be able to achieve a success that very few people have been able to achieve, whether they have a limitation or not. To be able to look back on your life and know you were successful at your work, but even more so in life, is a tremendous gift you can give yourself.

If you are able to keep your family, finances, relationships, and spiritual and physical needs all spinning effectively, then you have achieved success. But to have a successful career at the expense of your family and relationships is not success, and does not define a Raging Sloth. Your goal is to live a better, more extraordinary life because of the balance you have been able to maintain.

To accomplish this balance, I want to look at five specific plates in more detail: your work, your physical life, your social life, your mental state, and your spiritual life. These are the main five plates you need to balance. Within these plates, there may be numerous smaller plates to spin, which is where you need to watch your balance. But by gaining a better understanding of these plates, you can garner a better understanding of what you have to balance and why.

WORK

The sloth is a sloth. It does not get to choose to be anything other than a sloth. But the sloth doesn't take this lying down, most of the time. They do not get the luxury of neglecting the important tasks in life. The sloth still has to live, eat, mate, and survive. In other words, it has to work, and it has to get the job done, in order to continue living the life it has created.

The same is true for the Raging Sloth. You may have to work, unless you are independently wealthy, in which case you can skip to the next step. For most of us this is a necessary plate we need to balance. Most of us do not get the option to live off a trust fund. You may be supporting a family, and you may even be the sole provider for your family. Or you may have a family to raise, a house to keep up, and other duties assigned to you in this life.

You cannot let your limitation get in the way of your being able to support your loved ones. So what do you do as a Raging Sloth who has others relying on them in some fashion?

You may not be at the job you love or a place you feel called. You may want to do more, you may want to be the person you have always seen yourself as in your dreams, but the bottom line is you do not feel like you have what it takes to accomplish the goals you have outlined. This attitude may lead to avoidance of a new task or project because you fear failure.

This is a battle I deal with on a daily basis. On good days I truly feel like I can conquer the world. I get work done, I spend time with my family, and I believe I can accomplish anything placed in front of me. But on bad days, days when the pain is overwhelming, the doubts can become almost as crippling as the pain.

Can I really start a business? How can I compete with others when I struggle at getting out of bed? Nothing I do is worthwhile. I am useless. Who would want to listen to someone who has these thoughts? I stare at my goals while curled up on the couch in pain, doubting I can ever get them off the ground if my condition never changes.

The thoughts become a constant tirade of self-doubt, which can consume my day. It is challenging. Some of the thoughts are legitimate, attempting to balance my limitation with a successful career.

These are the times when I have to be brutally honest with myself and try to remember my definition of success. My limitation is a reality in my life and my work, and I need to do my best in creating an environment where I can keep the plates spinning as consistently as possible.

When you are working within a limitation there are two things you need to remember. The first is you may still have to work a job, even if your current circumstances are not ideal. If this is the case, you still need to work hard, learn what you can, and press forward in your current position. There still may be opportunities to grow your strengths or practice your skills.

When I was working at my corporate job, I would not hesitate to take the young new consultants into an informal coaching arrangement. They loved being able to ask questions and receive one-on-one attention. It also allowed me the ability to refine my coaching skills.

Always look for opportunities to advance your skills, regardless of your circumstances. This may be a time when you need to sharpen your saw for your next adventure.

The second thing you need to remember about working with limitations is you need to look at your journey as an intentional wanderer. Do not let any experience you have go to waste, but use it to grow, learn, and understand how your own habitat might be unfolding. Even if you do not understand your purpose at the time, what you're doing right now may be the vehicle you need to take you to your habitat.

You must also be realistic with your limitation. If your work is becoming too difficult, look for different arrangements at work. Talk with your boss or human resources. Take the necessary time off to recover. Make sure work is not adding to your stress or causing other plates in your life to be neglected. Look at your work through a realistic lens and address it appropriately.

PHYSICAL

Even though the caricature of a sloth is somewhere between a rock and a snail, keeping our bodies in tune and in shape is extremely important. The only way I have been able to reduce my use of pain medication is to work out, eat right, stay fit, and fight off the pain—but this has never been an easy process.

I also understand all the people who are telling you "just work out more, you will feel better." It is irritating and frustrating for you. But you need to ignore them. You need to do this for yourself, because you desire to create a better adventure for your life.

If you are not maintaining some level of physical health, other plates in your life can easily begin to wobble. You will not enjoy your success, your money, or being able to spend time with your spouse or children. This is difficult—believe me, I get it—especially when you feel your body is your enemy, but regardless of your limitation, keeping your physical self balanced is absolutely paramount.

You may not be able to run a triathlon, but you do what you can do. It may be simple stretching, lifting light weights, or going for a short walk. It does not matter what you do as long as you are attempting some routine. If that means simply eating right, avoiding certain foods or drinks, then that's what you accomplish in order to bring your life back into balance.

I'd been somewhat athletic well before my hip went out, so this was a difficult transition for me. I could not participate in many of the activities I did in the past, but I learned to adapt. I discovered that riding a bike does not bother me, so I mountain bike as much as possible.

Snowboarding also doesn't bother me, after the initial falling-all-the-time phase, so I snowboard as much as possible. There are some days, however, when I can only do one run on the snowboard because my body is not up to the activity. I do what I can, and I'm not afraid to experiment with new activities.

We like to hike as a family. I know that if I go on a long hike, I am going to pay a painful price. But it's a risk I take because time with my family is worth the pain, you may have to add up your risks. You may pay a price for certain activities; just add up the costs and make sure it is worth it.

You need to stay in tune with your body. Know when you can take the risk and know when you need to rest. But go into every day leaning toward the risk-side. Wake up knowing that you're going to lean into the day with full intensity. This attitude can have much-needed positive reinforcements about how you look at life.

What I also learned through this process was working out is therapeutic for me. I came to understand that if I work out consistently and stay in shape I won't have to take medication. Participating in activities gave me the strength to endure the pain on a daily basis (for the most part—on really bad days I still need medication). But overall, the stronger I felt, the better I could attack the day.

During extended periods of time when I was unable to exercise, the pain got worse, I became more irritable, and I struggled with life in general.

When my body is in tune, it helps me better keep my limitation in tune. I feel like I am the one in control of my pain instead of the other way around.

Our body is all we get. We do not get to exchange it for another, or most of us would have already made this return long ago. We need to take care of it as much as possible, especially if our bodies are the source of our limitation. We need to ensure that we are keeping this plate balanced at all times; if it falls, then our other plates will quickly fall afterward.

SOCIAL

If you are a Raging Sloth, then the social part of your life may be the most difficult to manage. You need to make sure you keep your social plate spinning proportionately. This includes your internal family relationships as well as your external friend relationships.

Ironically, sloths tend to be solitary animals, but this should not be the case for you. In fact, you may not even have a choice in this manner. Most people who deal with chronic pain do not want to be around other people when the symptoms are flaring. I will admit I am grumpy, cranky, and probably not very pleasant to be around, and that is usually on a good day.

But when you insert pain, social interactions of any kind can be challenging at best. I do not like who I am and the way I act in pain, but that does not excuse my actions. The pain makes it extremely challenging to be around others, but I know I have to persevere in this area because I cannot live this life on my own.

The reality of my life is I have a wife who needs a husband, and three teenage kids who need a father. I have to be present; this is not an option. But to keep this plate spinning, I had to drop my expectations of the type of husband and father I wanted to be and come to the acceptance of the type of husband and father I could be.

I thought I would be the dad in the backyard playing basketball, throwing a football, or running with my kids. But this would never be the case. It was not bad; I just had to find the activities I could do with my kids. I could snowboard, ride a bike, hike, and rock climb.

On more painful days, we go to a movie, the zoo, or play card games. These activities cause less pain than the more physical ones that pound on my hip.

These were the activities we did, when I could. This was never the life I intended, but the point was I was spending time with my kids. I was making time with my wife. They loved it. I'm not sure if they liked the activities, but they tolerated them because they do love spending time with their dad.

For my wife, it has probably been a little more difficult. She's had to care for me like a child while I was bedridden for a month, in a body cast going from my chest to my ankles. She has watched me suffer through physical therapy, learning to walk again, and the constant pain, which can shift my moods widely. Not exactly what she signed up for when she said "I do."

I have to be intentional about communicating with Erica. Since I am a guy, this activity is more difficult than it would appear. When the pain comes, I tend to retreat into myself. I shut myself off from my family, relationships, and the world.

This is partly because I'm a dude and this is what we do, but I also know I am not pleasant in these moments—if I simply avoid people, then I can avoid problems.

If I do not open my mouth, then I cannot say anything offensive. Also, my skin is very thin during this time because I'm constantly agitated by the pain. If I close myself off, then I cannot be angered.

I retreat into myself because I'm fighting off the pain and it's draining all the energy I possess. But my wife sees this as me pulling away from her, which is never my intent. I have to be able to communicate with her on what I am feeling and experiencing.

For the sake of our relationship, I need to tell her if I am having a bad day. She gets it and is fine with it, and she makes her little adjustments and we continue throughout the day. By telling her what I'm going through she realizes that my mood has nothing to do with her, or that it's not because of anything she did, which is huge. She is obviously a strong woman and can deal with what I go through. She has proven her endurance for years. But she needs a temperature check every now and then of where I am on any given day.

Relationships are tough in general. They become even more complex when you are trying to overcome obstacles in your life. But you need them, and you cannot avoid them because of limitations. You will never make it alone. I cannot even imagine what my life would be like if I did not have my wife, kids, and friends around to support me and hold me up during those times I have been unable to support myself.

You need to keep your social plate spinning. This will be the plate you will want to walk away from first because of excuses you tell yourself. But dig deep, endure, and make sure you are creating space for your relationships to prosper. You really do not want to live a life with a limitation on your own.

MENTAL

The next plate we need to keep spinning is our mental and emotional state. When you are dealing with a limitation, life gets tough, no question. Simply getting out of bed in the morning can be a monumental task that seems burdensome and overwhelming.

This is why you need to be extremely careful about letting your mind take you into dark places during your more challenging times. When you are suffering and in pain, and dealing with a limitation you don't want, you have to be very careful in balancing your mental state. Most days you are walking a fine line between clarity and depression.

It is easy to have the "Woe is me!", "Why me?" or "What did I do to deserve this?" moments. These thoughts and statements can begin you down a dangerous path. I am a part of several online chronic pain groups, and the negativity I constantly see on those pages is concerning. I get it, you need to vent at times. Life is difficult. We have already established our circumstances suck.

But dwelling on your pain, your suffering, and how people don't understand and mislabel you does not benefit you at all. The negativity you bring upon yourself in the midst of your challenge is another added weight you don't have the ability to carry.

You have to resist. Remaining positive is the most difficult yet necessary gift you can give yourself. This is the plate you have to be strongest in spinning. Nothing good comes of your time in the negative places, and you need to beware of the time you are spending with the doubts and disappointments.

Sandi Krakowski, when reflecting upon her own chronic pain, stated: "When we identify ourselves with a condition and take on its identity rather than our own, a dark, dark place is waiting for us. We can feel trapped, isolated and even succumb to thinking death would be a better option than having to live out this thing any longer."

Like most people in pain, this has been one of my more difficult struggles—mainly because when I'm in pain and I work hard to overcome the pain and get my life into a pretty decent place, but then another wave of pain comes back, it makes me want to say, "Why bother?"

I get doubts that I cannot do anything. I get depressed that I do not have any contribution to society. Sometimes I don't know how I am going to do my job, support my family, be a husband or father. I have had the thoughts that death would be better than having to live another day in pain.

The doubts and demons come quickly and they scream with a megaphone. While I allow myself to have bad days, I try extremely hard not to let myself dwell in these places for very long.

About a year after my initial reconstruction surgery, I realized I was going into a deep depression. At 27 years old, I struggled to walk and was living every day in pain, and I was not equipped to deal with this loss on any level. I went too far into the dark places of life, and it was almost devastating.

Luckily, I was able to recognize what was happening and I pulled myself out of the mire with the help of friends and family. But it was a valuable lesson that taught me not to let myself dwell in the dark places.

You need to keep a watchful eye on this plate and make sure you are balancing it effectively and efficiently. This plate is much better to spin when you have the help of others. Their encouragement, strength, and guidance will allow you to keep this part of your life in balance.

SPIRITUAL

The last part of your life, probably the most important, is your spiritual life. You have to be able to keep your spiritual plate spinning regardless of your circumstances. If you lose sight of God's purpose and design in your life, then what you try to produce will be for selfish reasons. You will also easily lose sight of a greater purpose your limitation can serve.

In coming to terms with your limitation, a natural part of the process is to doubt God and wonder why he would let this happen to you. These are normal thoughts, and contrary to what you have been told, they are good thoughts to have. The point is not to linger very long with your doubts. The most difficult part of your journey will be having enough faith to trust that God is working through these painful times.

A couple of years after my initial surgery, I hit rock bottom mentally, physically, and especially spiritually. I was raised in the church, served in the church, minored in religion in college, and taught classes at church. I knew in my head what it meant to serve God, but it was a different reality in the midst of writhing pain.

I was at the point of turning my back and simply walking away. I could not deal with it anymore. I could not sing songs in church, listen to the pastor, and hear everyone's chipper stories. Numerous people praying for my healing with no results was devastating. I did not see the point anymore.

But God redeemed me and began to show me a different path. It was not the path I was traveling on, or even a path I knew existed, but I had to have faith in what He was doing and trust the path that was laid out before me. (You can hear more about how I viewed God in the midst of pain at http://www.ramblinlife.com/my-personal-story-of-pain/)

I would not be writing this book or have the amazing opportunities to discuss engaging obstacles with people if it weren't for the pain I have suffered. This is Christ's power at work in me through the process.

We have to be able to keep our eyes on the spiritual plate and keep it spinning no matter what our circumstances. You do have an amazing purpose and an amazing story. Do not let your limitations deny your voice and prevent the world from seeing your amazing gift.

If you can at least keep the five plates spinning in a proportionate and appropriate manner, you have taken a gigantic leap in keeping your life in balance. You are also on the path to becoming a Raging Sloth and learning how to live a more balanced life on your terms.

14

THE SERIOUS BUSINESS OF PLAY

Resurrecting Your Fun Side

It might reasonably be maintained that the true object of all human life is play. Earth is a task garden; heaven is a playground. ~ G.K. Chesterton

I will gladly admit I have always enjoyed play. From organized sports like football, basketball, and rugby to riding bikes, snowboarding, rock climbing, and throwing the Frisbee. My youth was filled with play, and it was an aspect of my life I gladly brought into adulthood.

When the pain came, play disappeared from my life. Part of the issue was the amount of energy I was putting into addressing my pain. I had very little to expend on any type of play at the end of the day. But when I really dug deep into my loss of play and I was honest with myself, I also realized that I no longer understood how play fit into my life.

One Christmas, about a year after my first reconstruction surgery, my wife bought me a kayaking trip down the Great

Falls River in Virginia. At any other point in my life, I would have been ecstatic to kayak down a river. But as I stared down at the gift certificate, there was nothing but fear in my heart. I was paralyzed at the thought of putting myself in a possibly pain-inducing situation. Or the realization I simply could not accomplish this endeavor.

There were no thoughts of fun or joy, only questions of "Can I do this?", "Will I hurt myself more?" and "Do I even have the strength to attempt this activity?" In the immortal words of B.B. King singing "The thrill is gone" kept popping into my mind. The activities I had come to love growing up now terrified me because of the additional pain I thought I might incur if I participated.

Needless to say, with play out of my life, I was not a very fun person. My life only consisted of work and dealing with pain, and neither was a very fun prospect at the time. It would take several years for me to relearn how to play and reintroduce myself to activities.

My reintroduction to play would also require a tribal intervention because I was not venturing into these activities alone. My dad got me back into riding motorcycles and experiencing the joy of the wind in my face.

I am eternally grateful for Steve pulling me out to rock climb when I didn't think I would ever be able to scale a wall again; for Scott, who would get me out mountain biking and snowboarding; and for Glenn, who, for some reason, was willing to suffer through my attempt to play a round of golf, and yet never complained.

It was also beneficial for me to rediscover activities that were enjoyable yet required little physical exertion. I could spend days in my Jeep off-road with the top down, as this is always an enjoyable activity. I got back into shooting and archery and taught myself woodworking and how to work on cars.

The point is, a major factor in being a Raging Sloth is the actual raging part. Otherwise, we are just sloths. We can never lose sight of the fun and play which ignite our very souls. These are probably even more paramount to our lives and to our success.

When play was removed from my life, I was nothing more than a robot. It is difficult to explain, but it was as though something had died inside of me. I could go to work and function, but there was no light. There was no joy shining out of my life.

WHY WE LOST PLAY

There is a general issue with losing play in our society. Many individuals move past their youth and into adulthood, and feel that play is a part of their lives they're supposed to leave behind. They get married, buy a house, have kids, and pour themselves into their career. We live with the idea that a responsible life is a life devoid of play.

In general, those individuals who have lost play are not a happy lot. Even though they know, buried somewhere deep inside of them, they long for play—they light up at a certain joke, or a brief moment of whimsical play—they lost how to incorporate play into their lives.

When you are living with a limitation, this loss of play can be devastating. Similar to my own situation, you somehow manage to work play out of your life. Depending on your situation, you may not have time or energy for play anymore.

The pain may be too overwhelming, and so you push play out of your life. The burden of life itself is too great and does not allow any room for extracurricular activities. Working and living require all your energy. You do not know where you will be able to pull any extra energy for play.

I remember those times when play would sneak up on me, and my heart would be filled with pure joy and bliss. There were several occasions during this time when we would get together at my friend Kellar's house with all our college buddies. We would sit around the fire until the late hours of the night, laughing until our stomachs hurt. This was a glaring reminder of how important it was for me to reintroduce play back in my life.

THE IMPORTANCE OF PLAY

We all need play in our lives. This is not just opinion; there is scientific research that shows the multifaceted benefits of play in our lives. One of the researchers leading the way is Stuart Brown, MD, who is the founder of the National Institute for Play. (Why did I not know this place existed, and how do you get a job here?)

Brown stated: "Play is a state of mind, rather than an activity. Remember the definition of play: an absorbing, apparently purposeless activity that provides enjoyment and a suspension of self-consciousness and sense of time."

Researcher Jaak Panksepp has shown that "active play selectively stimulates brain-derived neurotrophic factor (which stimulates nerve growth) in the amygdala (where emotions get processed) and the dorsolateral prefrontal cortex (where executive decisions are processed)." For us nonscientific types, Panksepp is stating that animals who play are better equipped to navigate the world, are better adjusted socially, and are smarter.

When you don't play, your brain "shrinks." You lose cognitive skills, your imagination is diminished, and problem-solving skills become more difficult. Brown states: "When play is denied over the long term, our mood darkens. We lose our sense of optimism and we become anhedonic, or incapable of feeling sustained pleasure."

Without a doubt, play is important in our lives. Although the scientific research is a reassuring backdrop to justify our fun, I doubt any one of us would question the healing properties of a good ole belly laugh with friends. Play should be one intricate thread tightly wound in the complex webbing of our lives. If we are living, then play should not only be a part of our lives, but we need to be empowered to play in our lives.

THE POWER OF PLAY IN PAIN

This empowerment is even more paramount in the life of someone living with a limitation. If you suffer from chronic pain, are constantly caring for another individual, or are living with a disability, a tremendous amount of your energy is being diverted to engage your obstacle on a daily basis.

If you keep going at this pace, keep draining this amount of energy without ever recharging your cells, you will eventually burn out. You cannot sustain an abundant life solely focused on your limitation.

While there are many reasons for the average individual to play, if you are living with a limitation, there are three very important reasons to play. The first is that play keeps you in the game of life. Play keeps you off the couch and outside your head where the negativity might creep in, and you end up feeling more optimistic.

Many people living with a limitation are constantly teetering on the edge of depression. When you are suffering, you want to pull away and fight this battle yourself. But play, in any form—a walk with friends, a game of cards, or watching a movie or sporting event with others—gets your brain moving, intertwines you with others for social interaction, and gets you back into the world.

I cannot even begin to count the number of times my wife committed us to some activity that I did not want to participate in. I was tired, I hurt, I didn't know anyone, and—I could always come up with a million more excuses. Besides, I never knew how I would feel when the event arrived.

But almost every time, after the party or event, I would feel rejuvenated and alive. Left to my own devices, I would probably live like a hermit. But the interaction of play with others is what has kept me relatively sane for all these years. Play is what makes me feel most human. As mentioned in an earlier chapter, play can keep me from the dark places of my mind. Play reminds me of the joy that can be found in life.

The next reason we must play is that it opens up our creativity and helps us clear our thoughts so we can keep our focus on what is important. With a limitation, you can get too much inside your head, focus too much on your problem, or indulge in self-pity. Play opens up your mind to many more opportunities and pathways to discover, which could never happen sitting on the couch.

On days when I am able to be more active, a bike ride is revolutionary in clearing my head and giving me the ability to get back to a project or task with greater vigor than before. In my less-than-active times, doing a crossword puzzle or playing a mind game on my phone is a great distraction. These activities stretch my mind to clear my thoughts and address problems I might be struggling with to work through them with more ease.

The more we lay on the couch and check out of life. the more we are restricting our creativity. Play keeps our creative juices flowing. and through this process may be how we discover our purpose. Play is essential in keeping our mind open in order to see the opportunities all around us.

The last reason play is necessary is that it's a great distraction. Like I mentioned before, when you are living with a limitation, too often you get stuck inside your thoughts with all your problems. Your thoughts can become consumed with all your pain, what you cannot do, and the life you lost. These are not productive. They do not serve you well at all, and let's face it: no one wants to hear you complain all the time. Engaging in play is a phenomenal way to get your mind off your limitation.

You have to realize there are times in your life, because of your limitation, when you simply need to lose yourself in an activity. Forget your limitation and remember that life is good. Remember how much life can be restored to your soul through that side-splitting evening with friends.

I experience this blissfulness when I snowboard. I'm not sure what it is about the activity, or if it's because I have done it for years and my muscles and nerves simply know how to react, but on days when I'm up for it and I begin gliding down the mountain, my body kicks into autopilot mode and my brain essentially shuts off. In this euphoric moment, I'm not thinking about my pain, my struggles, my challenges, or really anything. I'm simply in the moment, letting my body do what it has been trained to do. The cleansing effects of the activity are indescribable.

By the end of a couple of runs, my mind is clear, my body is cleansed, and I am ready to tackle anything that comes my way.

I experience the same blissful mind-clearing times over a good dinner with close friends, playing music with fellow musicians, or simply enjoying a board game with the family.

All these activities suit to remove me from my current existence of pain and remind me of all that is good around me.

Play is the only activity, albeit in many different forms, that has kept me human, in the game, and engaging with people. The importance of continuing to engage in play while living with a limitation is absolute in the life of a Raging Sloth.

HOW WE GET PLAY BACK

If play is important, then how do you incorporate it back into your life? Being a Raging Sloth is not just about career success, but it is also about life success and living life with gusto.

If you are going to begin the process of getting play back in your life, begin with remembering what used to bring you alive. What did you enjoy when you were younger or before the obstacle was placed in front of you? How can you bring this activity back into your life?

If you are unable to incorporate some of those activities into your current life, then experiment. Find new activities that you might be able to enjoy or are similar to old activities.

If you have kids, you have built-in play machines who will gladly point you down a path of play. If you don't have kids, go find a few to hang out with; it should only take about a minute for them to get you involved in one of their imaginary games.

Part of me wishes my children never had to endure watching their father suffer. But I know I am a far better person because they have challenged me to grow and given me a purpose beyond self-pity and sitting on the couch. Although there are days when it is exhausting trying to keep up with them, it is always worth it.

When you have figured out your play, then put it in your plan. You want to be intentional about times of mindless play—not competitive sports, which can leave you angry—but simple play.

By being purposeful about your times of play, you want to eventually move to a point where play is *infused* in your life, not simply some activity only reserved for the weekends. Why can't you make a meeting more playful? A doctor visit? Time with friends? The opportunities are limitless.

Life is awesome and made to be enjoyed, so make the effort to ensure play is a regular part of your regimen.

LETTING LOOSE

You also need to be able to allow yourself to let loose. This may be the more difficult part. During those times of pain when I turn inward and try to avoid people, I need to resist the urge to avoid engaging others. There are times when letting loose can be the most freeing experience you have. It can recharge you in ways you never imagined.

Each year, this is my philosophy going into our Knights of Heroes camp. The campers don't come to camp to see mentors who sit around and do nothing. I go into each camp knowing I'm going to let loose, even though there will be a price to pay physically at the end of camp. But God always seems to give me some special grace to let loose with my body during this week.

I'm up at 5 a.m. leading a Bible study, and then it's off to mountain bike, rock climb, or river raft. I talk with mentors throughout the day about their campers and spend the evening in deep conversation with the campers about their loss or struggles in life. Then I'm off to bed late at night to start the whole activity over again the next day. It is absolutely and amazingly exhausting.

By the end of the week, I can barely see straight and I'm completely drained. But there is an indescribable peace and calm in my soul because I've let loose, I've played, and I've given back.

Giving back is probably the greatest way for you to play by engaging in random acts of kindness. Let giving to others become a part of your daily routine. It can be extremely freeing and can lift many burdens off your shoulders.

There are many opportunities for you to intertwine times of giving back with play. It is another method of taking the focus off yourself, and it can be an extremely enjoyable act of play. When you are helping others and giving back, your limitations may not seem as heavy, which is always a great improvement to your life.

PLAY LIKE A RAGING SLOTH

Remember, you are not a sloth. You are not content to simply sit on the couch and let life happen. You are not content to be defined by your limitation. You are a Raging Sloth; you have a fire within you that gives you a desire for more than the obstacle that stands in front of you. So go rage. Go have fun and enjoy all that life has to give you.

No matter how much success you achieve, if you are not enjoying your time and your experience in this life, then what is the point? How can you get your family involved, how can you engage your friends more closely, and how can you not only live, but play like a Raging Sloth?

15

A TRUE RAGING SLOTH

Commitment to Working Hard

No! Try not. Do. Or do not. There is no try. ~ Yoda

Even though the sloth may seem like a lazy animal and was unceremoniously given this title, they still do not have the luxury of sitting on a branch while other animals bring them food and take care of their basic needs. Sloths still have to get their food, raise their young, watch out for predators, and thrive in life as best as possible. Being sloths does not mean they are exempt from doing the hard work necessary for life.

The same holds true for Raging Sloths. Even though you are living with an obstacle and don't live like others, your limitation does not excuse you from the hard work necessary to reach your goals and be successful.

You cannot expect anything to be given to you because you have a limitation. No one cares. This may sound harsh, but it is the truth. If you want to succeed and meet all of your goals, you are going to have to work hard. In some cases, you may have to work harder than those around you.

I have learned over the years that the average individual cannot even begin to grasp the depths of chronic pain. My wife, who has lived by me and watched me suffer for the past eighteen years, does not understand my pain. My family and close friends do not understand my pain. When you have not suffered in intense pain over long periods of time, it's difficult to comprehend the plight of someone who has. Why would I expect anyone on the periphery of my life to understand or comprehend what I experience?

No matter what type of words or imagery I use to explain how I feel, most people cannot fathom my experience. They don't understand why I can't work some days or not show up to an activity.

I had one individual come up to me at one point when I was in devastating pain, and tell me, "I know how you feel. I stubbed my toe last week and boy, did it hurt!" I was honestly speechless. If this is the type of pain others think I experience, then no words would be sufficient to describe the depths of my suffering.

The only way I can even convey what I experience is to tell someone to carry a fifty-pound weight out in front of them all day long. Not on your back—that would be too easy. You have to carry it out in front of you.

Throughout the day, you do not get to put it down to attend to all your normal activities. As the day progresses, let me know how much more difficult each activity becomes. At the end of the day, let me know how utterly distracting and exhausting it was to carry the excess weight. Then you might begin to understand what every day is like for someone who suffers from chronic pain.

This is why I cannot expect anyone to understand what life looks like for me and why I work hard within my own habitat. This is the place where I blaze hard when I can, and rest when I can't. My definition of hard work will not look like everyone else's, but it fits into my habitat. The definition is conducive to my goals based on my limitation.

You do have to realize this is a slippery slope. You have limitations, some of which may restrict you from putting the time necessary into a project or goals. You may feel your limitation is excluding you from having to work hard. Some days, getting out of bed is a triumph; so you think you do not have to work as hard, or you do not have the ability to work hard.

You also may be in a situation where you do not want to set yourself up for failure, which is a completely reasonable feeling. You need to realize, however, that success is not defined by working an eighteen-hour day. Remember, you have already defined success and your goals on your terms. Now you have to put in the necessary work to achieve these goals.

HARD WORK IN ACTION

I saw a great example of hard work, perseverance, and strength in my own son Jude one summer while we were mountain biking with my other son, Dylan, and my friend Scott. We went out early in the morning, starting out at around 9,200 feet of altitude. For the first hour, I think we were constantly going uphill with only a few minor dips to ease the grind of the upward ascent.

When we finally got to our first good descent, Dylan went down first, followed by Jude. But when Jude began his descent, he was flying like a wild fox with its tail on fire. I don't believe I have ever experienced firsthand anyone descending a mountain at such lightning speed who was not competing in a professional race.

Jude was breaking the sound barrier at an uncontrollable pace. I am sure my eyes have never been as large as they were that day, as I stared in paralyzed silence and fear. It was the type of situation where you know something bad is about to happen, but you are helpless to change the outcome. It was a surreal moment, as life was moving in slow motion and hyper speed at the same time.

As Jude neared the bottom of the hill, he had three options: hit the sign at the bottom of the path, hit the log to the right of the sign, or, if he was lucky, regain control and veer off to the left and continue down the trail. Unfortunately for Jude, he chose option two and hit the gigantic log to the right of the sign.

Upon impact, he and the bike went flying up in the air. Now the positive side to this escapade was there was nice soft ground with long grass on the other side of the log. The unfortunate part was the large log hidden underneath the nice soft grass where Jude proceeded to land on his back. Then the bike landed on top of Jude like something from a Saturday morning cartoon.

By the time I raced to the bottom of the hill, Jude was jumping up and down, holding his back, and desperately gasping for air like someone who's just had the wind knocked out of them.

After a few minutes of calming him down, being the brilliant father I am, I didn't want to miss this opportunity for a little life lesson with my son. You know those moments where you think you can teach your children in the midst of adversity.

Once Jude was calm enough and could breathe normally, I asked him, "What did you learn from this little adventure?" In my mind, I was thinking I was father of the year for always trying to teach my children lessons, and I was expecting a response about controlling your speed.

But Jude's response to my questions was far from what I was anticipating. He looked up at me with tear-stained eyes and, short of breath, to state loudly, "My brakes don't work!" More than surprised by the response, I immediately looked at Jude's bike and realized his brakes were indeed faulty and would not press fully against the tire. My poor son had white-knuckled it down the hill, squeezing the brakes with all his might to no avail.

Scott and I spent some time trying to get Jude's brakes fixed in order to avoid him breaking the sound barrier down another hill. We then headed back out on the trail, for we still had another five or six miles ahead of us.

Throughout the rest of the ride, Jude was still struggling. He kept on having to stop, kept on needing water, and was, in general, moving very slowly as we made our way along the trail. I kept on pushing him, encouraging him, and prodding him until we finally made it to town where my wife met us with the car.

I couldn't quite understand why this bike ride had been so difficult for Jude, other than thinking he never fully recovered from the fall. Jude is very athletic and capable of out-riding all of us on any given day with his natural endurance.

But the answer came to me when I was loading Jude's bike up on the bike rack. I noticed his back wheel was not spinning freely. It only moved when I forced it with my hand. It was at this point that I realized Jude had completed the rest of the trail with his brake calipers rubbing up against the tires.

When we had fixed Jude's brakes to avoid another rapid descent, we had overcompensated, and they were pressing down on the tire rim. Basically, Jude had been riding the rest of the trail at about five times the resistance the rest of us had been riding. I was immediately in awe of my son.

What impressed me most about what Jude accomplished is that even though there was some weeping and gnashing of teeth, he never gave up; he never quit. He never threw his bike down, sat down, and pouted or said he was not going any farther.

He was limited by the bike he was on and the massive bruise he had on his back, but Jude kept going forward to the end, even though it was extremely difficult, somewhat painful, and probably not a lot of fun from his perspective.

Even more impressive was Jude getting back on a bike. We were going out for another bike ride the next day and I asked Jude if he wanted to come. He excitedly said yes, except he was not going to ride the bike of doom; he never wanted to ride that bike again.

He went back out with us the next day and the next. What I found out that day is Jude has a tremendous amount of inner strength I didn't even know about, something that he has not fully realized. The beauty about inner strength is we all have more than we realize, but it only reveals itself in times of perseverance.

INNER STRENGTH

You need to remember the inner strength and perseverance you have when it comes to different challenges and obstacles in your life. I am amazed by the enormous amount of strength you have to fight through during these times—even when you don't think you have any strength left to finish. If you can just dig deep, learn to fight, and press through, I think you will be amazed at what you can accomplish and endure in your own life.

I have many days where I'm not sure how I'm going to make it through—when the pain is overwhelming, nothing I do alleviates the discomfort, and my entire source of energy is being drained simply by my attempt to act human. If you are in a similar situation, what you have to realize is you, like Jude, have a tremendous amount of inner strength.

Your life may seem like you are living at five times the resistance as those around you. But you have the ability to endure hardships, challenges, and struggles that would bring the average individual to their knees.

At the end of particularly draining days, I am always amazed that I made it through. I know I have this inner strength that is beyond anything anyone around me knows or comprehends. I do not know if those around me know how much I have to tap into this inner strength either.

But my strength is what keeps me in the game of life, and it is what keeps me human. It is also what I tap into in order to be successful, for I know I can endure far more than those around me.

Like Jude's struggle on the bike, my adventure may not be easy and may require more inner strength than I thought possible. Even though I may be moving slowly, I am still digging deep and moving forward. This is how you reach your destination.

Victor Kiam is quoted as saying, "Even if you fall on your face you're still moving forward." It may not be pretty but your inner strength is what is going to keep you moving forward.

Be very proud of what you endure and use this power. Use this inner strength on your good days and channel it back into your life. Realize the power inside of you and invest it back into your relationships, your own life, and your career.

You can accomplish far more than the average individual because every day is a battle for you—but a battle you are victorious over. Give yourself a pat on the back, relish what you have endured, and apply this energy toward your future.

WORKING WITHIN YOUR HABITAT

The real defining point of this process is having the ability to work within your habitat. If you are not working within your habitat, the simplest tasks will seem overwhelming. You are attempting to balance a trying limitation with a job that may also be draining your energy. The end result is always challenging. But when you work within your habitat, it can transform how you approach your job and your ability to endure the hard work.

When you work within your habitat doing what you love, you will begin to realize that your limitation will not seem so limiting. The pathway to success will become clearer, and you will be able to work within your limitation to become successful. Life in general will become more enjoyable. But it will be up to you to achieve this balance in your life. You have the strength to make your life amazing.

HARD WORK EVALUATION

The Companion Guide will walk you through and help you understand what your life looks like with your limitations, passions, and definitions of success and how all of this ties into the ability to work hard in accomplishing your goals.

Is work a nine-to-five job, a weekend job, a split-shift job, or some combination of all three? Is it working for yourself, a partner, or a large company? What does this specifically look like for you? You need to be as specific as you can in understanding the rhythms of your life, apply this to your plan, and then execute as precisely as possible.

I am able to work pretty hard on any project, as long as I have control over the schedule. My biggest issue is trying to keep up with someone else's schedule. This almost always frustrates me because I never know what my days are going to look like. I'm still reluctant to volunteer for activities because I don't know how I will feel when it is time for the event.

Through the processes I have laid out in this book, I have realized that the more in control I am of my schedule, the more productive I become. This has been a successful strategy for me to work from. It allows me to work hard, and I generally feel like I accomplished quite a bit at the end of each day.

I feel productive, which is huge when battling a limitation every day. It has taken me many years to figure this out based on my work, my pain, and the rhythms of my life.

This is the direction in which you need to be pushing your life. You need to create your plan and then execute full force against it. It will not be easy and it will not come easily. You will have to put your blood, sweat, and tears into your goals and projects.

Nothing is going to be handed to you in this process. But you will transform your business and life, and create your own brand of success by working hard in your habitat to accomplish your goals. Otherwise, you will still live in an old world, on a false journey, thinking success should just be given to you because you are awesome—or worse yet, because you have a limitation.

Even though your success will not be handed to you, you still deserve the success you attain. It is not for someone else to obtain; it is for you. Make the plan and then work hard on it so you can create a better adventure and live full force in the extraordinary life you created.

16

A LIFELONG RAGING SLOTH

Thinking Long-Term

Long-term, we must begin to build our internal strengths. It isn't just skills like computer technology. It's the old-fashioned basics of self-reliance, self-motivation, self-reinforcement, self-discipline, self-command.
~ Steven Pressfield

If you are going to be successful and create a life on your terms, there are two final aspects of this life you need to concentrate on. The first is being laser-focused, and second is long-term thinking.

By being laser-focused, you are less likely to flow in and out of many projects. The projects may change each year, but for the current goals you are attempting to accomplish, you must stay completely focused. You cannot be successful if you attempt to juggle multiple projects that are taking your time and expending energy you do not have.

This is why your plan is important. Your life is a distraction. You live a life with a limitation or obstacle constantly in the forefront of your mind. You do not have the ability to neatly pack away your limitation in your closet when not needed. Every morning you need to get up and look at your purpose, remember your goals, and be laser-focused in committing whatever energy you have to moving just one step closer to your goal.

If you do not have a goal or focus, you will either wake up with no purpose, which will not serve you well and can have long-term ramifications, or you will jump on any bandwagon that comes your way and makes you feel good. Both of which are nothing more than a distraction. Your success in life, careers, and relationships will be guided by your focus.

You also have to think long-term. If you know your limitation is not going to change, then you need to plan and visualize how your success is going to be mitigated in the long run. This is important so you do not simply seek a quick fix to get out of a current situation.

This may have to happen under certain circumstances in order to get back to your habitat. But in creating your goals, defining success, moving to your habitat, and working hard, you are moving through each of these steps with long-term goals in mind.

You have to remember that you are working with limitations, so it will probably take you longer to accomplish your goals than the average individual. But you have planned for this and it is a part of your goals and life plan. You have built this contingency into your goals and your definition of success.

Because it will take you longer to accomplish your goals, you have to be in this game for the long haul. Your journey will be difficult, it will not come easily, and it will be fraught with roadblocks. If you are only thinking short-term, then you will turn around, give up, and quit at every point where you get tripped up along the way.

If you never give yourself the option of giving up or going back to a right-side up life, then you have no choice but to keep moving forward.

ALWAYS BE FLEXIBLE

Becoming a lifelong Raging Sloth also requires flexibility in how you approach your plan. Motivational speaker Tony Robbins once said, "Stay committed to your decisions, but stay flexible in your approach." This is exactly the mindset you need in order to succeed—and the reason why I dedicated an entire chapter to this topic. You need to have your goals in place, but the road you take to reach them may change dramatically several times.

I've had several ideas for books bouncing around in my head for years. This whole process began because I wanted to write a book—but not this book. I had never even thought about writing a book that addressed chronic pain and success. But as I was moving closer to my goals and fulfilling my dreams, this is the book that began to come together.

I needed to be flexible enough to put my other projects on the back burner and explore where this book was going to take me. It was still within my goals; the content was still within my life plan, so I began to pursue this endeavor. As

Tony mentioned, I was still committed to my decision, but I was staying flexible in my approach.

I also have to be flexible in my approach to life. I have made big plans and I fully expect to execute them. But I have no idea what each day will hold. All I can do is keep an eye on the future and live fully in each day. It is all I have.

I don't know if the pain will come back worse, if another body part is going to jump ship on me, or if other tragedies may fill my life. All I can do is live for today and make the most of what this day gives me. I choose to make it awesome!

A LIFELONG RAGING SLOTH

By the end of my life, all I can do is look back and hope all those single days added up to something awesome because I had a vision of where I wanted to end up. You are in this for the long haul. You are not looking blindly at your current circumstances. You are living in the moment while looking ahead at what will be. This allows you to achieve your success.

If you are not looking at the long haul and keeping your focus on what you eventually want to achieve, you are going to jump ship at the first sign of danger. The danger, the trials, and the challenges will come. You want to focus on the horizon during these times so you are not sidetracked or tempted to go back to a "safer," seemingly more comfortable life. You are a Raging Sloth, and a Raging Sloth may change courses many times, but they never turn back.

CONCLUSION:
LIVING AN UPSIDE-DOWN LIFE

You have brains in your head and feet in your shoes.
You can steer yourself any direction you choose.
You're on your own and you know what you know.
And you are the one who'll decide where to go...
~ Dr. Seuss

Much like the sloth, you have chosen to live your life and turn every aspect of it upside down. Now you need to embrace it dearly and live it out majestically. This is the life you have been given, and you can transform your life and live it to the fullest if you choose to live your life upside down.

Your temptation is always going to be the desire to live like others—to live your life right-side up, to choose a path of success behind someone else, or to try to emulate the life of someone else. I ran back to an old environment because I thought it was safe and comfortable, only to discover it was neither.

As humans, we all struggle with identity and the questions of, "Do I have what it takes?" and "Am I good enough?" We always want to know we are good enough to get the job done.

When you are living with a limitation, this question gets amplified because you always have the other question of "what if?" in the back of your mind. What if I did not have to live with chronic pain? What if (fill in the blank) had not happened to me? What if I had more energy?

These questions can haunt us, and more importantly, they will distract us from our designated path. These types of questions will make you want to live life like everyone else, which is impossible. Your life will never be happy, complete, or successful as long as you are attempting to live your life right-side up.

Let's change the questions floating around in your head to reflect a new attitude. What if I live life to its fullest? What if I engage my limitation head-on? What if I do live my life upside down? Remember, you are the hero, and it is time to change the narrative.

YOUR UPSIDE-DOWN LIFE

When I was still trying to live a normal life, believing in the back of my mind the pain would someday go away, I was always struggling to live my life right-side up. This baneful pursuit took me out of a life I had created upside down and put me into a right-side-up life. I was working in the business world, waking up every day and putting on my tie and dress shoes, and going into an office and pretending to be someone I wasn't.

I felt like every time I put on my dress clothes, I was putting on some costume to go perform someone else's show. For the longest time, I knew it was not right, but I was paralyzed by not knowing how to correct the situation.

This may be you right now. You may be going into an office where you do not feel like you belong. You may be lying in bed struggling to understand or find your purpose. You may be wrestling with the loss of your career or dreams due to your limitation. Resist the urge to turn your life right-side up and embrace the opportunity to live your life upside down.

This is not an easy process, and it was extremely difficult to get my life back to the upside-down world, but it was very much worth the effort. You will not simply wake up one day and choose to live different. It will begin with a transformational choice. But will require you every day when you wake up to choose to live different, to live a better adventure.

Remember, you are a warrior. You are a fighter. If you are reading this book you have a 100% success rate at getting up off the mat. You have proven your strength and resilience in life. Now it is time to apply it to your purpose.

When you commit to this process you will find your place of comfort. This is my place of comfort. This is the place I was born to live. This is how I was made to survive, thrive, and be successful. This is what you were made to accomplish, and you will find your purpose and joy in living a life on your terms.

YOU ARE A RAGING SLOTH

This book was created as a guide to help you move your life to the upside-down life, a life built and defined on your terms in your understanding and pursuit of success. You have been given a plan, a direction to move your life forward.

You sit on the precipice of a decision. Do you choose the more difficult, more rewarding path of living your life upside down, on your terms? Or do you stay in a rut living some-one else's life, which will never get ANY better or get you to where you want to live?

You may need to go back through this book several times. You will have to make adjustments and be flexible. You need to learn more about yourself, make your plan, create a vision, and find a pathway to reach your definition of success. You need to be able to give yourself grace and be flexible with your plans based on your limitations.

But you can do it. You can achieve your goals. More than achieving your goals, you can live a more wondrous, adven-turous, extraordinary life by living it on your terms.

You are not alone. You are not the first to enter this habitat and try to live upside down. You may be the only one around you who has to live this way, but you are not alone. You have just joined the community of Raging Sloths.

APPENDICES

DISCUSSION QUESTIONS

Chapter 1: The Sloth's Predicament

- What is your dream? What adventure did you hope to pursue when you were younger?

- How has your adventure been turned upside down?

- Have you been able to reconcile your dreams and your reality?

- How do you need to rewrite your epic adventure?

- How do you see yourself as the hero in your new story?

Chapter 2: When Life Gets Turned Upside-Down

- How has your life been turned upside down?

- How has your life, your health, and your relationships been affected by this obstacle?

- Do you ask yourself, "Why did this happen to me?"

- Do you currently have any vision of what life looks like with your obstacle in the way?

- Has your obstacle turned your dreams and adventure upside-down?

Chapter 3: Denying Your Limitations

- How would you describe your limitation to a friend? What adjectives would you use in describing this obstacle?

- When describing your limitation, do you shrug it off like it is not something of interest or worth discussing?

- Is there any chance your limitation may be taken away, healed, or removed? If so, is this hope beneficial or detrimental to your success?

- Have you fully contemplated the ramifications of your limitation in all parts of your life? How does it affect every part of your life?

- Describe in detail how your limitation has affected your life. How has it changed your dreams, your relationships, your self-image, or your career?

Chapter 4: Step One – Engaging Your Limitations

- What is your greatest fear about engaging your limitation?

- Why do you think you need to engage your limitation?

- How has not engaging your limitation created issues or more challenges in your life?

- What are three ways you can engage your limitation?

- Have you taken the time to discover your purpose? What is it?

- How do you think engaging your limitation can lead to more freedom in your life?

Chapter 5: Step Two – Defining Success

- Are you building your life around another person's definition of success?

- How do other definitions of success cause stress and frustration in your life?

- What is your greatest challenge or fear about defining success on your terms?

- Describe five ways your life could dramatically change by defining success on your terms.

- What does success look like for you when you engage your limitation?

Chapter 6: Step Three – Knowing Your Passions

- Can you easily identify your passions?

- Are there passions in your life you know you should not pursue? Passions that are better relegated to hobbies or weekend activities?

- Have you discussed your passions with your fellowship to get their thoughts on your pursuits?

- How are you using your secondary passions as a way to unwind and remember to enjoy life?

- What are the first three steps you need to take to turn your passion into a pursuit?

Chapter 7: Step Four – Adjusting Your Habitat

- Do you feel uncomfortable in your current habitat but do not know why?

- Explain the discomforts you feel in your current habitat.

- Describe your perfect habitat, built on your terms, for your limitations, with your dreams.

- Is this habitat a slight adjustment to or a major move from your current habitat?

- What is it going to take for you to adjust your habitat?

Chapter 8: Step Five – The Fellowship of the Raging Sloth

- Do you think a community of support around you is beneficial? Why or why not?

- Name three people in your life who can support you in your journey.

- Name three people you can reach out to, outside your community, who could be a support to you in your journey. These can be mentors, like-minded individuals, people whom you respect because of their knowledge, or leaders in their respective industries.

- How can you strengthen your current fellowship around your journey to success?

- How can you reach out to be a support to someone in their journey?

Chapter 9: Step Six – Entering the Danger Zone

- What have you not been willing to risk in order to achieve success?

- What area of success do you avoid but know is a danger zone you need to enter? Is it public speaking, reaching out to strangers, pushing your product, or another activity that gives you a knot in your stomach when you think about it?

- What is keeping you from entering your danger zone?

- List five ways entering your danger zone will be beneficial to your success.

- What tools, education, or experience would be beneficial to you in order to prepare you to enter your danger zone with more intentionality and purpose?

Chapter 10: Step Seven – Shifting Weight

- In what way do you keep yourself from being flexible when it comes to your limitation?

- How can you be more flexible in your life? How do you need to be more flexible?

- What will flexibility look like in your life? Write out three ways you can be flexible with yourself on any given day.

- How do you need to apply some grace in your life? Are you hard on yourself and your failures? What would this grace look like to you?

- How are you giving yourself room to fail on the pathway to success? The failures will come, but we need to make sure they do not derail us from our path.

Chapter 11: Step Eight – Owning Your Inner Raging Sloth

- In what areas do you compare yourself with other individuals?

- Why do you lack confidence in these specific areas?

- What is the single greatest area of resistance you face in becoming a Raging Sloth? Write this obstacle down. Then create a pathway to overcome your resistance. How will you overcome this obstacle?

- How can creating a life plan based on your obstacles guide you to a better path of confidence in your own success?

- Make a list of characteristics that make you the best you. What gifts, talents, abilities, and experiences are unique to you and you alone?

Chapter 12: Step Nine – Eliminating Excuses

- What is the greatest excuse, or what are the greatest excuses, you use in your life because of your limitation?

- Do you use any of these excuses as a crutch or a reason to not succeed?

- How can incorporating your limitation into your life plan eliminate those excuses in your life?

- In what way do you really need to own your existence and own who you are on your way to becoming a Raging Sloth?

- List any other major excuses you have been using in the past, and next to each excuse, write out how your life plan will eliminate it from your life.

Chapter 13: The Balance of the Sloth

- Is a balanced life something attainable to you, or something that resonates in your life?

- How has your limitation affected the balance in your life?

- Which aspects of your life (physical, mental, emotional, spiritual, or professional) are most out of balance?

- What will be your greatest challenge in creating a balanced life?

- How will your limitation hurt or help you in the process of creating a more balanced life?

Chapter 14: The Serious Business of Play

- Have you all but eliminated play from your life because of your limitation?

- What are some of the activities you enjoy doing but have not engaged in?

- When you create your life plan, what does play look like in your life?

- How do you think play will benefit you in your pursuit of a successful life?

- What are some ways you can integrate play and flexibility to create a more meaningful life?

- How can you incorporate your passions into your play time?

Chapter 15: Commitment to Working Hard

- Have you been using your limitation as an excuse to not work hard?

- Are you concerned that because of your limitation you will not be able to work hard enough to be successful?

- Look at your life and your limitation realistically. What does "hard work" look like for you? What can you realistically do on any given day to reach your goals?

- How can you make adjustments on a daily basis to work hard, but work within your limitations (i.e., adjust your schedule on more challenging days)?

- What is it going to take for you to succeed in life based on your limitation?

Chapter 16: A Lifelong Raging Sloth

- When you look at your life, your goals, and your limitation, are you building a long-term plan?

- What are your long-term goals for success? How are you building your plan to achieve these goals?

- Are there any aspects of your plan that may appear shortsighted or are not contributing to your long-term goals?

- What safeguards do you need to put into place in your life to ensure that you stay committed to your goals in the long term? (Relationships, deadlines, goals, etc.)

- What does your path look like in pursuit of long-term goals? How is this different than trying to achieve something in the short term?

- What do you have to do to achieve your long-term goals? (Education, seminars, training, etc.)

Conclusion: Living an Upside-Down Life

- What does your upside-down life look like?

- Can you fully embrace the Raging Sloth?

- Are there others you know who need to be brought into the Raging Sloth community?

- How are you keeping yourself accountable to stay in your habitat?

- What is the one way you are going to celebrate becoming a Raging Sloth? (Go big—you deserve it!)

ACKNOWLEDGMENTS

To my wife Erica, I simply want to say thanks for all of the support even through difficult times. You are a ray of light in the dark times of my life. Thanks for always being there. Thanks to my children, Dylan, Jude, and Presley, for enduring all of Dad's sloth discussions, for always supporting me, and being the most amazing kids on the face of this earth.

To my mom, dad, and sisters for creating a solid foundation for me to live. Without your guidance and love I could never have become a Raging Sloth.

Glenn Nevill for always being there for me. You are like a brother, and I will always be grateful for your friendship. You have given me the ability to work beyond my means and do more than I ever imagined.

Scott Timothy for all our harebrained conversations. After about a thousand different ways to go, I was finally able to land on something. Thanks for the talks; I look forward to every single one and to many more.

Matt Parker for your continued encouragement. You have always had the right words to say when I needed them most. Your encouragement and support in all my pursuits have been very life-giving.

Steve Harrold for always believing in me and giving me a place give back. You have always challenged me to risk and have made me a better person. Thanks Suzanne for your final suggestions and edits you are a patient miracle worker.

Thanks to all my other friends, supporters, churches, and colleagues who have supported me through this process. The ability to experiment and bounce ideas off of you has been instrumental.

ENDNOTES

Introduction:

1. The Police, "King of Pain," *MP3 Lyrics, http://mp3lyrics. com/Lyric/1994889/*, accessed February 17, 2016.

2. "Megatherium," The Sloth Sanctuary, http://www. slothsanctuary.com/about-sloths/giant-ground-sloth/, accessed January 8, 2016.

3. Knights of Heroes Foundation, http://www. knightsofheroes.org.

Chapter 1: The Sloth's Predicament

1. Walt Disney, Brainy Quote, http://www.brainyquote.com/ quotes/quotes/w/waltdisney163027.html, accessed January 2, 2016.

2. Carolyn Gregoire, "Happiness Index: Only 1 In 3 Americans Are Very Happy, According To Harris Poll," Huffington Post, http://www.huffingtonpost.com/2013/06/01/happiness- index-only-1-in_n_3354524.html, accessed February 13, 2016.

3. Dan Miller, *48 Days to the Work You Love*, (Nashville: B & H Publishing Group, 2010), 20.

4. "AAPM Facts and Figures on Pain" The American Academy of Pain Medicine, http://www.painmed.org/patientcenter/ facts_on_pain.aspx, accessed February 13, 2016.

5. Reviewed by David Zelman, MD, "Depression and Chronic Pain," WebMD, http://www.webmd.com/depression/guide/depression-chronic-pain, accessed February 13, 2016.

6. "9 Ways Chronic Pain Impacts Quality of Life," ShareCare, https://www.sharecare.com/health/chronic-pain/health-guide/chronic-pain-management-cmp/9-ways-pain-impacts-life#slide-10, accessed February 13, 2016.

7. Radha Chitale, "How Chronic Pain Gets Into Your Head, *ABCNews*, http://abcnews.go.com/Health/PainManagement/story?id=4249610&page=1, accessed January 21, 2016.

8. (https://www.hss.edu/conditions_emotional-impact-pain-experience.asp)

9. Malcolm Gladwell, *Outliers*, (New York: Little, Brown and Company, 2008), 19.

10. Peyton Manning, *Wikipedia*, https://en.wikipedia.org/wiki/Peyton_Manning, accessed February 17, 2016.

11. Chelsey Sullenberger, *Highest Duty* (New York: HarperCollins, 2009).

12. J.K. Rowling, *Wikipedia*, https://en.wikipedia.org/wiki/J._K._Rowling, accessed March 1, 2016.

13. *Unbroken*, directed by Angelina Jolie. 2014; Moore Park, Sydney, New South Wales, Australia. Fox Studios.

Chapter 2: Life Getting Turned Upside-Down

1. "C.S. Lewis Quotes, " *Essential C.S Lewis, http://www. essentialcslewis.com/2015/12/26/fact-quote-quiz-1226/* accessed February 17, 2016.

2. "What Is A Sloth?," Slothville, http://www.slothville.com/ what-is-a-sloth/#.VsSrUPEp3b0, accessed November 4, 2015.

3. *The Matrix*, directed by The Wachowski Brothers, (Warner Bros., 1999), DVD.

Chapter 3: Denying Your Limitations

1. "Oscar Wilde Quotes," *Goodreads,* http://www.goodreads. com/quotes/194182-to-regret-one-s-own-experiences-is-to- arrest-one-s-own, accessed February 17, 2016.

2. "William Shakespeare Quotes," *The Tragedy of Hamlet, Prince of Denmark*, OpenSourceShakespeare, http:// www.opensourceshakespeare.org/views/plays/play_view. php?WorkID=hamlet&Act=1&Scene=3&Scope=scene, accessed February 17, 2016.

Chapter 4: Step One – Engaging Your Limitations

1. "Helen Keller," *WikiQuote*, https://en.wikiquote.org/ wiki/Helen_Keller, accessed February 17, 2016.

2. Sandi Krakowski, "How Chronic Pain Made Me A Stronger Person", *Entrepreneur*, http://www.entrepreneur. com/article/250593, accessed February 13, 2016.

3. Sandi Krakowski, http://www.arealchange.com/.

4. "Ralph Waldo Emerson Quotes," *Wisdom Quotes*, http://www.wisdomquotes.com/quote/ralph-waldo-emerson-8.html, accessed February 17, 2016.

5. Emily Esfahani Smith, "There's More To Life Than Being Happy," *The Atlantic*, http://www.theatlantic.com/health/archive/2013/01/theres-more-to-life-than-being-happy/266805/, accessed May 15, 2015.

6. Viktor Frankl, *Man's Search For Meaning* (Boston: Beacon Press, 1959), 119.

7. Frankl, *Man's Search For Meaning*, 105.

Chapter 5: Step Two – Defining Success

1. "Bruce Lee Quotes," *BrainyQuotes*, http://www.brainyquote.com/quotes/keywords/be_yourself.html#1kosfXAdf04JsM2Z.99, accessed on February 17, 2016.

2. "Success," *Dictionary.com*, http://dictionary.reference.com/browse/success?s=t, accessed December 14, 2015. (Italicize added)

3. Dr. Linda Seger, "Five ways to define success," *Fairfax County Economic Development Authority*, http://www.fairfaxcountyeda.org/five-ways-define-success#sthash.PhQhPh2y.dpuf, accessed December 14, 2015.

4. Courtney Spritzer and Stephanie Abrams, "With Social Media, Fakes Are a Real Problem For Your

Business," *Entrepreneur,* http://www.entrepreneur.com/
article/233677, accessed December 20, 2015.

5. Michael Hyatt, "How To Develop The One Trait Essential
For Success," *MichaelHyatt.com,* https://michaelhyatt.
com/developing-persistence.html, accessed December 21,
2015.

6. John Maxwell, *Leadership Wired,* June 2003.

7. *The Raging Sloth,* http://www.ragingsloth.com/
companion_guide.

8. "SMART Criteria," *Wikipedia,* https://en.wikipedia.org/wiki/
SMART_criteria, accessed February 17, 2016.

Chapter 6: Step Three – Knowing Your Passions

1. "Dead Poets Society," *Wikiquote,* https://en.wikiquote.
org/wiki/Dead_Poets_Society, accessed February 17, 2016.

2. I asked my sister to review my "artistic interpretation" when
I was describing artists. This was her reply: "Walking through
the museum, I could appreciate the vibrant use of color. The
way the artist captured light and the texture of the brush
strokes, whether it be in the rendering of the human face by
Van Gogh or a still life with fruit by Cezanne. I was in awe of
the varied ways that artists created landscapes, from the lumi-
nous mountains of Bierstadt to the color-soaked water lilies
of Monet." I had to laugh since it only further displayed the
disparity between my understanding of art and that of someone who can truly appreciate what they are viewing.

3. *Jerry Maguire*, directed by Cameron Crowe, (TriStar Pictures, 1996), DVD.

4. J.D. Salinger, *The Catcher in the Rye*, (New York: Little, Brown and Company, 1951).

5. *American Idol*, created by Simon Fuller, (2002; Glendale, CA: Fox Broadcasting Company).

6. *The Raging Sloth*, http://www.theragingsloth.com/companion_guide.

Chapter 7: Step Four – Adjusting Your Habitat

1. "Maya Angelou: Her quotes, poetry and prose," *CBSnews.com*, http://www.cbsnews.com/news/maya-angelou-quotes-poetry-and-prose/, accessed February 17, 2016.

2. Aaron McHugh released his first book, *Fire Your Boss: A Manifesto to Rethink How You Think About Work*, in 2016. It can be found at http://www.amazon.com/Fire-Your-Boss-Manifesto-Rethink-ebook/dp/B01B2025VI/ref=sr_1_1?ie=UTF8&qid=1455738602&sr=8-1&keywords=aaron+mchugh. Leith McHugh runs Brave Beauty at http://bravebeautyb2.weebly.com/.

3. "Sloth," a-z animals, http://a-z-animals.com/animals/sloth/, accessed January 4, 2016.

4. "61. Maned Three-toed Sloth," *EDGE Evolutionary Distinct & Globally Endangered*, http://www.edgeofexistence.org/mammals/species_info.php?id=63, accessed January 4, 2016.

5. "Two-toed Sloth, Choloepus didactylus & Choloepus hoffmanni March 2009," *San Diego Zoo Global*, http://library.sandiegozoo.org/factsheets/sloth/sloth.htm, accessed February 5, 2015.

6. Graham Rapier, "Mark Zuckerberg and Hoodies: How Casual is Too Casual?," *Inc.*, http://www.inc.com/graham-rapier/how-casual-is-too-casual.html, accessed February 17, 2016.

Chapter 8: Step Five – The Fellowship of the Raging Sloth

1. "Henri Nouwen," *Wikiquote*, https://en.wikiquote.org/wiki/Henri_Nouwen, accessed February 17, 2016.

2. Mark 2:1-12, Paraphrased.

3. John Ortberg, *Everybody's Normal Till You Get To Know Them*, (Grand Rapids, Michigan: Zondervan, 2003), 44–62. Ortberg did a phenomenal job retelling the story of the paralyzed man, and was inspirational in this paraphrase.

4. Ortberg, *Everybody's Normal Till You Get To Know Them*, 52.

5. "C.S. Lewis > Quotes > Quotable Quotes", *Goodreads*, http://www.goodreads.com/quotes/443803-the-next-best-thing-to-being-wise-oneself-is-to, accessed February 17, 2016.

6. "New Zealand national rugby union team," *Wikipedia*, https://en.wikipedia.org/wiki/New_Zealand_national_rugby_union_team, accessed February 10, 2016.

7. "The Greatest Haka Ever," Youtube video, https://www.youtube.com/watch?v=yiKFYTFJ_kw.

8. Maggie Hendricks, "Breaking Down the Haka Before All Blacks Play in Chicago," *USAToday.com*, http://www.usatoday.com/story/sports/olympics/2014/10/28/all-blacks-haka-usa-chicago/18078559/, accessed March 2, 2016

Chapter 9: Step Six – Entering the Danger Zone

1. Kenny Loggins, *Danger Zone*, http://mp3lyrics.com/Lyric/1569659, accessed February 17, 2016.

2. "What Is A Sloth?," Slothville, http://www.slothville.com/what-is-a-sloth/#.VsSrUPEp3b0, accessed November 4, 2015.

3. *Fearless* by Eric Blehm is a great book on what our heroes have endured during service.

4. http://www.scorreconference.tv/. I have no affiliation with nor attended the SCORRE Conference. Research to find which public speaking forums might be most suited to your danger zone.

Chapter 10: Step Seven – Shifting Weight

1. John Maxwell, *Intentional Living: Choosing a Life That Matters*, (New York, Center Street, 2015), 399.

2. Jeff Goins, *The Art of Work*, (Nashville: Nelson Books, 2015), 118.

3. http://www.theragingsloth.com/companion_guide.

Chapter 11: Step Eight – Owning Your Inner Raging Sloth

1. "Popeye", *Wikiquotes*, https://en.wikiquote.org/wiki/Popeye, accessed February 17, 2016.

2. Ephesians 2:10, Paraphrased.

Chapter 12: Step Nine – Eliminating Excuses

1. Proverbs 23:7 KJV.

2. Amy Nordrum, "What's Your Excuse?," *Psychology Today*, https://www.psychologytoday.com/articles/201407/whats-your-excuse, accessed January 23, 2016.

Chapter 13: The Balance of the Raging Sloth

1. "John Wooden Quotes," *AZ Quotes*, http://www.azquotes.com/quote/480817, accessed February 17, 2016.

2. Guillaume Billet, Lionel Hautier, Robert J. Asher, Cathrin Schwarz, Nick Crumpton, Thomas Martin, Irina Ruf, "High morphological variation of vestibular system accompanies slow and infrequent locomotion in three-toed sloths," *The Royal Society Publishing*, http://rspb.royalsocietypublishing.org/content/279/1744/3932, accessed February 2, 2016.

3. "What Is A Sloth?," Slothville, http://www.slothville.com/what-is-a-sloth/#.VsSrUPEp3b0, accessed November 4, 2015.

4. Sandi Krakowski, "How Chronic Pain Made Me A Stronger Person", *Entrepreneur*, http://www.entrepreneur. com/article/250593, accessed February 13, 2016.

Chapter 14: The Serious Business of Play

1. G.K. Chesterton, "In Praise of Play," http://gkcdaily. blogspot.com/2013/09/in-praise-of-play.html, accessed February 17, 2016.

2. B.B. King, *The Thrill is Gone*, http://mp3lyrics.com/ Lyric/1953376/, accessed February 10, 2015.

3. Stuart Brown, MD, *Play*, (New York: Avery, 2009), 60.

4. Brown, *Play*, 33.

5. Brown, *Play*, 43.

6. Ibid.

Chapter 15: Commitment to Working Hard

1. Lawrence Kasdan, "The Empire Strikes Back", *IMSDB*, http://www.imsdb.com/scripts/Star-Wars-The-Empire-Strikes-Back.html, accessed February 17, 2016.

2. "55 Motivational Quotes That Can Change Your Life," *Brightdrops.com*, http://brightdrops.com/best-motivational-quotes, accessed March 2, 2016.

Chapter 16: A Lifelong Raging Sloth

1. "Steven Pressfield Quotes," *AZ Quotes*, http://www. azquotes.com/quote/236202, accessed February 17, 2016.

Conclusion: Living an Upside-Down Life

1. "Dr. Suess > Quotes > Quotable Quote," *Goodreads*, http://www.goodreads.com/quotes/22842-you-have-brains-in-your-head-you-have-feet-in, accessed February 17, 2016.

2. Tony Robbins, *Awaken The Giant Within*, (New York: Free Press, 1991), 123.

THE RAGING SLOTH
COMPANION GUIDE

Follow along *The Raging Sloth* with assessments, guides, and plans to help you become The Raging Sloth

IF YOU LIKED THE BOOK
YOU WILL LOVE THE EXPERIENCE
Join The Raging Sloth Community

Do you want to work directly with Eric Eaton?
Let Eric guide you through a transformational process of defining success and living life on your terms.

Imagine finding purpose and living an
extraordinary life regardless of your challenges.

You can join a coaching group, enlist in one of *The
Raging Sloth* courses, or join our online community.
Participants can join from anywhere in the world.

Find out more at
THERAGINGSLOTH.COM

Why keep living an ordinary life when you
can live an EXTRAORDINARY life?

BRING ERIC INTO
your business or organization

AUTHOR. COACH. SPEAKER.

Eric understands the challenge of finding the right speaker for an event, bringing the correct topic, and the importance of engaging the audience. As a consultant, pastor, and business leader, Eric knows the success of any event can easily hinge on the quality of the speaker.

Eric is keenly aware of the need to engage with the audience, equip them with practical takeaways, and provide a different perspective on creating a better adventure. He customizes each message and training to achieve and exceed the desired objectives of his clients.

Contact Eric today
to begin the conversation
ERICPEATON.COM

Learn more about
KNIGHTS OF HEROES:

www.knightsofheroes.org

ABOUT THE AUTHOR

Eric's desire is to help people create a better adventure in their own lives to live an extraordinary life. Through his writing, speaking, and coaching he helps people realize they are not alone in their struggles. He provides a path to live an extraordinary life regardless of circumstances by learning to live upside-down.

Eric started out early in his career blazing a quick trail of success as a consultant. However, he was sidelined by a hip reconstruction surgery, which left him in chronic pain at age 27. Eric attempted to continue his life as normal with his family, in consulting, and as a senior pastor. But after many failures, he realized he could not live life like everyone else. He could only live an abundantly crazy life if he learned to live upside-down on his terms.

Eric wants to show those who live with limitations that their lives have meaning and purpose. Through his leadership, speaking, and writing, he is committed to helping people find their own path to a better adventure. Eric and his wife Erica live in the mountains of Colorado and are blessed with three awesome teenagers.

Connect at: EricPEaton.com

Made in the USA
Lexington, KY
20 July 2016